RUNAWAYS

RUNAWAYS

BY
ANNA KOSOF

Franklin Watts   1977   New York / London

Library of Congress Cataloging in Publication Data

Kosof, Anna.
  Runaways.

  Includes index.
  SUMMARY: Describes the life of runaway
youths, situations they are trying to escape, and
programs that try to help them solve their problems.
  1. Runaway children—United States—Juvenile
literature. [1. Runaways] I. Title.
HV741.K67   362.7'4   77–7234
ISBN 0–531–01293–X

For Rick, Stefan, and my mother

Acknowledgments

This book could have never been written without the immense help that so many people graciously offered me. I am very deeply indebted to the New York Police Department for permitting me to spend time with the runaway unit of the police force. I would like to single out Sergeant Greenlay and Officer McGinniss, who spent a great deal of time riding around with me in search of runaways. These men were instrumental in my research, as they shared with me a good amount of information that would have been impossible for me to ever experience first-hand. I would also like to thank all the runaways who were so patient with me, telling me of parts of their lives that were very painful to recall. My special appreciation goes to the runaway programs that permitted me to do research within their facilities. And I would not be fair if I did not thank my editor, who helped me throughout this project with concern and patience. Also, thanks to all the people who put up with me in the process, and Melvin Van Peebles, at whose insistence I wrote this book.

Contents

RUNAWAYS

Introduction

By Honorable Birch Bayh

Member, U.S. Senate (Dem.-Ind.)
Chairman, U.S. Senate Subcommittee
to Investigate Juvenile Delinquency,
Committee on the Judiciary

As many as one million young people run away from home each year. What are the reasons? What are they seeking? Answers are not necessarily clear. We do know, however, that of these youths over 188,000 were arrested for this offense last year—an "offense" which is only applicable because of the person's minority age status. It is commonly referred to as a status offense.

The runaway problem has continued unnoticed for many years because it is a silent problem, far less dramatic than most of the other ills that affect our young people. Runaways are not criminals; they are confused boys and girls who are over-burdened with personal, family, or school problems and decide to leave home. They deserve our help and understanding, but instead they have been treated like criminals, with indifference, hostility and even incarceration.

This decade's runaways are far different from the "hippies" and "flower children" whom we observed with deep curiosity in the 1960s. The runaway of the 1970s is not looking for spiritual freedom, an end to the Vietnam War, or the right to smoke pot. This decade's young person is fleeing a personal

1

war—that of drug abuse, alcoholism, family disinvolvement, and often, especially in the case of many females, physically abusive parents. Tragically, social workers in some areas point out that incest and other forms of child abuse are cited by 40 percent of teenagers and even younger children as their main reasons for running away.

Some runaways attempting to locate a safe harbor from home problems soon discover they are in serious personal danger out on the streets and further compound their problems. Too often they become the victims of street gangs, hardened criminals, and drug pushers. Testimony developed at the hearings of my Subcommittee to Investigate Juvenile Delinquency linked a portion of runaway incidence to the use of dangerous drugs and to petty theft, especially shoplifting. Runaways often have to sell drugs or their bodies to support themselves. Each year our streets are receiving a new supply of prostitutes. These young girls and boys are usually under sixteen, some only eleven or twelve. They seek food and shelter with the only means of work they can get—selling themselves. In this way, running away often serves as the young person's first contact with the criminal world and the police. For others, this fleeting moment of a superficial physical interlude is the only experience that even comes close to resembling the love that they seek.

The female runaway outnumbers the male by two to one. This phenomenon is sometimes thought to be due to our society's still active sexual discriminatory mores: the male teenager is allowed to "act out" his frustrations at home and on the streets more than any female. But, in many instances, the runaway girl is jailed "for her own protection."

If life on the street is unpleasant, the lot of the runaways is not much better after they are arrested or turn themselves in. Ex-runaways are a major part of the youth population in mental hospitals, reform schools, and detention centers. In fact, one-half of all patients in mental hospitals are under twenty-one, and of the children incarcerated in state training schools,

2

23 percent of the boys and 70 percent of the girls are confined for status offenses.

In *Runaways,* Ms. Kosof refers to the runaway experience as a "mirror of our social problems." This is so true—it is a dusty, chipped mirror that too often reflects all the ills of our society that we have laid on the shoulders of those too young to understand them, much less accept the accompanying responsibilities.

The Runaway Youth Act of 1974 that I authored and was successful in gaining $9 million for in 1976, attempts to deal with this critical national problem by helping young people come off the streets without police intervention, by returning them home, and by providing the child and his or her family with counseling services aimed at the root of the runaway's problems. The primary function of this law is to provide a place where runaways can find temporary shelter facilities and immediate assistance, such as medical care and counseling. Once in the runaway house, the young person is encouraged to contact home and reestablish a permanent living arrangement, if this is advisable. Professional, medical, and psychological services are available to these group homes from the community.

Most important, the shelters established under my act are able to provide counseling for both the runaway and family members after the runaway has moved to permanent living facilities. If counseling is not appropriate or feasible, information on where to seek more comprehensive professional help is supplied. Federal legislation cannot provide a solution to the runaway problem, but rather can encourage local initiatives and can provide some of the resources necessary for local leaders to do the job. The best prevention still resides in the home. Parents must watch for that door that is constantly closed—the door to both the young person's room and mind. Youngsters need the assurance that they are an integral part of the family unit. The ability to talk things over can never be given short shrift.

Anna Kosof conducted an extensive study of runaway centers, visiting and talking with those who sought shelter within these facilities. She observed that, "In the runaway centers, some of the kids go to school, others look for work, or go to a training school. Still others spend much of the day hanging out in their room talking to staff, answering phones, typing letters that come to the house, or raiding the refrigerator on an hourly basis. . . . [but] they all have one thing in common. There is always plenty of talking going on."

There is no question that as an alternative for our runaway and homeless youth, these shelter homes are beginning to fill a void by providing a warm environment where the young people can feel comfort and understanding and where they can hope to find some meaning or purpose in their lives. Hopefully, parents too will feel some comfort in knowing that their daughter or son is safe and under supervision.

There are still countless young people who need to be reached. In the last decade the number of juvenile suicides has tripled—it is estimated that thirty young people take their own lives daily. There is nothing that can be done to help these children who are now past statistics, but there is much that we can do to aid those who do not seek such a permanent method of escaping their problems.

We must continue to strive for improved juvenile confinement centers, improved court processes, and basic rights for children. As in the past, young people of the future will continue to disagree with their parents, rebel against society, and run—looking for something better. What happens to them tomorrow is a problem that we must work toward solving today. We must polish our "mirror" so that we will be able to see clearly the obstacles that burden our young people.

Ms. Kosof has captured and illuminated our picture of runaway youth—their daily pressures, their terrifying and heartbreaking experiences, and their search for ways to cope with the problems that complicate and confuse their young lives. Ms. Kosof's experience will help assure that those youth who have come apart from the community will instead become a part of it.

As we embark on our third century, contributions such as Ms. Kosof's book will help declare to the nation our commitment to young people who have been brought to the attention of the juvenile justice system. It is our responsibility to offer them a future worthy of anticipation.

Who Are the Runaways?

The runaways used to make the news. At one time they were famous. Not so long ago, in the height of the protests of the 1960s, young people of our country, almost as a unit, were rebelling. Haight-Ashbury and the Lower East Side were like magnets, drawing thousands of the rebelling young. The American cultural revolution had begun. Our sons and daughters were turning their backs on their parents, on traditional American values, on society, and on the government.

These runaways were America's flower children. They came from all parts of the country. They left the comforts of their middle-class American suburbs by the dozens. Dressed in jeans and sandals, sporting long stringy hair and no makeup, they left home to take part in the most celebrated social movement of this century. They ran away from material possessions and parental values, and turned to what they conceived of as a peaceful way of life. The Protestant ethic of hard work was rejected in favor of Eastern values. America's young had said no to America. They refused to become members of a capitalist society in which material possessions meant status. They refused to adhere to the sexual norms of their parents' generation. They accepted the invitation to belong to a culture whose greatest concerns were drugs, peace, and perpetual love-making.

When they left their homes, it was for very clear reasons. They rejected not only their own family's values, but those of a large part of the American cultural system as well. They left angry, often denouncing their families. They departed in groups, heading for their Mecca, hoping to get there by the grace of God. Some took the family car. Others took the bus, hitched rides with total strangers, or walked many long miles. Their departures made a statement about how they wanted to live and what kind of society they wanted to be a part of.

Most of them were white and middleclass. They left their parents confused, wondering what they had done wrong. The parents felt they had done their best—sent their children to the best of schools, dressed them in the finest clothes, and sheltered them in good homes. And now their children were leaving, over some principle or other, some concept labeled "the generation gap," a notion that they could not fully understand.

The runaways created a culture of their own, filled with a new vocabulary, a different style of clothes, and a life-style greatly modified from how they had lived at home. The parents were horrified, fearing for their children's safety, fearing that they'd lose them to another way of life, one that was clearly inferior to what they'd known at home.

The movement surpassed problems within individual families. The parents as well as the runaways were victims of a volcano that erupted in their own backyards. Helpless, parents hoped the explosion would be over quickly and their children would come to their senses and return to the life-style and values that they had known for all their lives.

Once they had wearied of their adventure, many runaways did return. But they weren't quite the same as when they had left; they had acquired some new values that tended to modify the old ones they were returning to. In that way, the runaways

7

of the sixties, our flower children, made their influence felt throughout American society. They opened our eyes to new possibilities, opened our minds to other ways of life.

The runaways of the seventies are different. They are not running away from values or protesting an undeclared war. They are not running away from a life-style or from the notion of the American dream. For the most part, they are running away from unbearable situations at home. They don't run away in two's or in groups. Usually they go alone. They come from all economic classes, but mainly from the lower or lower-middle-income families. In contrast to the sixties, when most of the runaways were white, those of the seventies come from almost all groups. There are whites, blacks, Hispanics, and though less often, Asians. Most of the runaways of the seventies are female, as many as 70 percent, some authorities say. They come from all parts of the country and from all kinds of areas, rural, suburban, and urban.

When I asked runaways why they had run away, the youngsters often cited a family argument as the reason. But the roots go far deeper than that. They often extend to a miserable home atmosphere resulting from such problems as divorce, alcoholism, or child abuse. Alcoholism in parents and problems associated with broken homes headed the list of reasons. We must keep in mind also that the number of broken homes is at an all-time high. The divorce rate has risen to one divorce for every 2.3 marriages. Often, terrible conflict between parents will leave a child torn and confused. While not all runaways come from broken homes, or have alcoholic or abusive parents, many come from families that have serious problems that have gone on unresolved for many years.

Some runaways come from families that seem to be healthy. In these families, I often found that there was a pattern where the child had "gotten into trouble" at an early age, and the problem rather than being resolved, was ignored or glossed over until the parents eventually felt helpless and unable to control their child's actions. Many of these situations became a cycle that could not be stopped. Their child got into trouble, punishments or beatings followed, the kid got into more trouble, more punishment was inflicted, and arguments and fights ensued. The parents became increasingly disappointed with their child, who in turn interpreted the disappointment as the parents' no longer caring about him or her. Eventually the kid ran away, feeling rejected, and unable to get out of the mess he or she was in.

Often, family fights that caused a teenager to run away have been sparked by the youngster returning home at night at what the parents considered an unreasonable hour. Or maybe he or she came home drunk. Many of the kids have been torn between what they knew their parents wanted and their own desire to be with a certain crowd of their peers, who put pressure on them to do things they knew their parents objected to. Often, the teenager considered the activities to be reasonable, but the parents didn't.

When the situation at home is basically good, most of the runaways return after a few hours or days. Those who run away and do *not* return have homes they don't want to return to. Either they feel unwanted, or the situation in the home is so unpleasant that they don't want to face it again.

Running away can serve any number of purposes for the teenager. Some run away for attention, as a cry for help. And at times the device may indeed help the parents to wake up and deal with problems they had been refusing to confront. Running away can also serve as a solution—if an immature one—to a home situation that the young person can no longer cope with. A great number of runaways have left situations where physical or psychological abuse has become intolerable.

These are the runaways of the seventies. They are fourteen, fifteen, or sixteen years old, but many of them look older than their age. They are a large group. It is estimated that more than one million young people across the United States run away each year. The number is increasing. More and more young people leave their homes. Facing desperate circumstances, having to find food and shelter on their own, many of them become vulnerable to the worst forces of street life, and turn to prostitution and crime to survive.

Clearly, the runaway problem involves complex social ills. It points to the enormous problems that we have in keeping families intact, to the immense economic strain that has been prevalent for several years, to the rise of alcoholism. The seventies have taken on a frightening resemblance to that era during the thirties we had hoped so much to forget, when child neglect and abuse was at its height, when children wandered the streets in droves, begging and stealing, fending for themselves.

It is the lives of the new breed of runaways that we'll be taking a look at. Their lives at home, on the run, and at the runaway centers. We'll also get a view of how they see their own lives, and how their parents have responded to their act of desperation.

In going about examining the problems of the runaways in our society, I had to ask myself what was the best way to get a true picture of the situation. My decision was to go to the source, rather than sitting in a library reading about runaways. I set myself the task of finding runaways and their families, and talking to them.

Most of the research was carried out in New York City and Boston, and I talked by phone to people from several other parts of the country. Aside from obvious regional differences, many of the stories of the runaways throughout the country were remarkably similar.

At first I spent some time talking to adults who have worked with runaways, such as workers from the runaway centers. Once I had a good understanding of how the adults viewed the kids, I set out to find the kids themselves. In this undertaking, the New York police were extremely helpful. They gave me permission to spend some time with the police unit whose responsibilities are finding and working with runaways.

While tagging along with the police, I got to talk to many runaways.

Once I had gotten to know the numerous runaway centers, I established a close relationship with many of the adults in charge. They gave me permission to talk to the kids in their centers, who, once they had come to trust me, seemed pleased to be helpful, and they in turn gave me names of other runaways who were willing to share their experiences with me. In all, I talked to about one hundred young people who had at one time or other been runaways, whether they had returned home, were living in runaway centers, or were still on the streets.

I talked to parents who had had to look for their children, or were still looking. Other information came from published articles. To record the interviews as precisely as possible, I conducted most of them with a tape recorder. I talked to kids alone as well as in groups. Overall I believe I was able to obtain a fairly complete account of what it's like to be a runaway, what the runaways are trying to escape, and where they can run to for help.

The face-to-face contact was at times painful. But in the light of the intimate contacts I established with the kids, their parents, and the authorities, and the information supplied freely and completely by many cooperative people, I believe I was able to capture the runaway experience. Now, I hope to convey the experience to the reader. I hope to be a good translator.

·2·

The Runaway Cops

The runaway unit of the New York Police Department is a special squad of plainclothes officers whose job is not to arrest law breakers but to hunt down young runaways, many of whom are aimlessly wandering the streets of the city. The runaway police are on the lookout for young people they encounter on the streets who show evidence of being runaways, as well as for particular runaways whose parents have reported them missing. Finding a particular runaway can be pretty difficult. Often the cops have no more of a clue than that "she has long brown hair and green eyes, she is five feet four inches tall, and her name is Linda Jones." Sometimes the anguished parents can supply a high school picture.

The runaway unit in New York came into existence after the tragic mass murders in Texas, where some thirty young boys were sexually assaulted and killed. Many of the victims, as it turned out, were runaways. And they are not the only runaways to be permanently missing. In response to those deaths and the increasing violence on the streets which the runaways, young and uninitiated, are exposed to, the New York Police Department set up a special unit for runaways. The "runaway

12

policemen" are specially skilled in working with the young, knowing how to talk to them. They also know how to call parents to say that their daughter is alive but that she should see a gynecologist. They can make arrangements for the return of a child. And they can buy dinner for a very hungry runaway who has no money. The cops in the runaway unit are like storybook neighborhood police, every kid's friend and big brother.

The unit is usually composed of seven police officers—two three-man squads plus the sergeant. Some part of the unit goes out daily in search of runaways. The staff includes a policewoman. And the current staff feels that a woman is necessary to the unit. At the time this book was being written, however, which was during New York City's financial crisis, the unit had been cut to only two men, a situation that lasted one year— from June 1975 to June 1976. The two men remaining were Sergeant James Greenlay and Officer Warren McGinniss, both of whom have histories of more than twenty years of service on the police force. I traveled with them.

On a typical night, policemen Greenlay and McGinniss begin work around 6:00 P.M. Always traveling together and always dressed in ordinary street clothes, they spend the evening driving a shabby unmarked car or walking around New York City's streets looking for runaways.

Their route is pretty much the same every night. They start at the Port Authority bus terminal at Forty-first Street and Eighth Avenue, not far from Times Square, then zigzag back and forth east and west downtown to Greenwich Village. They go farther downtown to the Bowery then zigzag back up again. Slowly cruising, always looking, stopping, speeding up, parking the car and walking, watching, and then back into the car, they are always alert for any sign that might lead to finding a runaway.

It is not illegal to be a runaway. A person can't be arrested for running away from home. However, under the present Family Court Act of the State of New York, law officers can

13

legally ask for identification and a statement of purpose from a young person who shows signs of being a runaway.

A lot of runaways are found in the Port Authority bus terminal. Many kids come to the city by bus. The runaway cops look for young people without much luggage, perhaps only a backpack or a small bag. Kids who run away usually travel light. On the streets, the special police look for kids who show signs that they are living a life of crime—prostituting or stealing. They look for kids who stand out in the crowd because they seem very tired or are dirty. Looking lost is a good clue for the runaway cops.

Once the officers spot a possible runaway, they follow and observe, they wait and watch. If the person's actions continue to be suspicious, the officers approach the person tactfully and ask for some identification to show that he or she is of age—eighteen in most states. If they are satisfied that the person has proper identification and is not a runaway, they politely let him or her go and say "Sorry for the bother." If, however, the identification looks phoney, or the person has no identification, then they may ask for the phone number of the parents to verify that the person is are who they say they are.

If the officers decide a verification is necessary, they ask the person to go with them to their office. The runaway unit's office is not in a police station, but a large, dull, sparsely furnished room with cubicles and a bulletin board full of pictures of reported runaways. There, the officers call the number given as the parents' number. By this time, having ridden a while in the car with the person, the officers usually have a good idea whether or not he or she is telling the truth; but whatever their speculations, they have to make sure.

When the call is made, one of three things usually happens. Often the parents will verify that the kid is on the streets with their permission. The second situation is one involving the more experienced runaways. They'll give a phone number of someone who is not a parent but who has been set up to

14

cover for them. That person will quickly supply information to the officers, telling them things only a parent would presumably know. In that case, even though the officers sense something fishy about the situation, even though they strongly suspect the person on the phone was set up, they'll often have to release the suspected runaway, lacking sufficient evidence to hold him or her any longer. This phoney identification process is commonly arranged by pimps who use juveniles as prostitutes. The pimps don't want the runaway returned home, since he would be losing a source of income for himself. And the runaway doesn't want to be returned home for the same reason he or she left in the first place.

The third possibility is that the lucky parent will shout with joy that their youngster has finally been found alive. If that happens, the officers will spend the rest of the night making arrangements to return the runaway to his or her family—sometimes over the runaway's protests. This is the time when the night seems productive, when all the searching, the miles of walking and driving, the hours of waiting and watching, become worth the effort for the runaway cops.

The runaway cops never know what the evening will bring. Some nights seem so long, so futile, spending hours cruising, walking, and looking, and turning up with not a single runaway. Other nights turn up several new "nomads" wandering the frightening streets of New York City. Some of the runaways know the policemen well. Some have been picked up and returned home as many as five or six times. The officers try to be social workers, try to work out arrangements that may be permanent. But often they find a runaway girl, say, only fourteen or fifteen, talk to her like a father, return her to her home, then pick her up a week later. "We pick up a lot of repeaters," Officer McGinniss says. "Each time we hope against hope that it will be the last time."

To help me in my research, the two officers in the runaway unit agreed to let me accompany them on their rounds. The first evening was one of those hot, humid summer nights that New York City is famous for. Here is an account of a sample evening for the runaway cops.

Sergeant Greenlay and Officer McGinniss barely get to work when the phone rings. The caller is a woman who refuses to identify herself. She is reporting the whereabouts of a prostitute who she says is a runaway. What a lucky break for us. That's going to mean not having to look for the runaway, just going to pick her up. It looks like an easy night for sure. The caller tells the officer about a very youthful looking girl who is working for the same pimp she does. She gives a detailed description of the girl and the clothes she is wearing: a tube top and orange pants. She works the streets in the late afternoon, the woman says, and can be found on the corner of Delancey Street.

I ask the officers why she is calling the cops on the girl. Officer McGinniss answers, "Well, the girl is most likely wife number two, who is getting close to being wife number one." The female caller has sounded sincerely concerned that the girl is so young and working the streets. The caller gives the police the exact address of the hotel where we can find the possible runaway.

Sergeant Greenlay, Officer McGinniss, and I get into the green car, but we notice there is very little gas. This is during New York's financial crisis. The police department gas stations are either very low on their supply or have no gas at all. Not taking time to get gas right then, we set out to find this young girl.

The police know the Delancey Street area well. They know the hotel, and they are familiar with the coffee shop on the corner where so many of the prostitutes' customers are picked up. We park the car, and start walking along the street. It is knee-deep in garbage, and rats run freely. The officers take a good look at all the girls, but none fits the description given us. "Maybe she's in the hotel," says Officer McGinniss. We all wait about ten minutes, the time it would take her to do her job.

We each stand at a different spot, covering all corners, but she never appears. We walk around for a while, feeling very defeated, and finally leave.

Getting back to the car, it becomes apparent that before we can go very far, we have to get gas. We proceed to one of the police gas stations. It has no gas at all. We learn that the only station in the city with gas is uptown at Eighty-sixth Street and Central Park West. Shortly, we find ourselves at the gas station, waiting in line with a dozen or so other police cars. Finally, we can fill up the tank. We feel relieved that we won't get stranded somewhere without gas.

We drive back toward Forty-second Street and start cruising around the Port Authority area. The officers are observing everyone they see. They drive slowly enough so they won't miss a runaway, but fast enough so they won't block the already congested traffic.

The officers seem to know every young person on the street. The prostitutes also know the policemen. They say "Hello," or give us a dirty look, or make some comment such as "When are you going to give up?"

Tonight, all the young girls on the corner are ones who have previously been picked up and who turned out to be too old to be runaways—too old, being sixteen in New York State. The age at which a person can be classified as a runaway varies from state to state. To the runaway cops, sixteen is too young to be considered of age. A sixteen-year-old, they say, cannot survive alone. They believe the legal age in every state should be eighteen.

We go into the Port Authority building to watch for the arrival of any new runaways. The bus terminal has its own police who work with runaways. The two units work closely together, but the Port Authority officers cannot leave the premises, so the two units serve quite separate functions.

The situation at the Port Authority is tricky and requires some special skills. The police are not the only people looking for runaways. Pimps are always on the lookout for runaway

17

girls (and boys as well, in the case of the pimps for male prostitutes, but there are far more girls picked up this way than boys) and wait to pick them up at the bus station. In fact, the pimp's operation has become quite sophisticated. As a trick to fool the young girls into going along with them, they station innocent-looking women, often women who look pregnant, in the terminal to pick up the girls. A nice, safe-looking woman approaches a frightened, tired, hungry girl and asks her if she'd like a place to stay and eat a hot meal. The woman behaves very much like an old-fashioned Christian missionary. Often, the girl accepts and finds herself for a day or two in pleasant, warm surroundings. She is given a place to stay and good food to eat. At that point, a nice, friendly man seduces her, becomes an authority figure to her, the father figure she needs. Then, once she feels part of the man's life and comes to depend emotionally on the relationship he offers her, prostitution is offered to her as the only way that she can remain a member of her newfound family. The pimp molds her into the image of a working girl. Within weeks she takes on the look that brings in business in the world of prostitution.

The Port Authority cops have a quick job to perform. They have to spot the girl and get to her before the pimp or the "pregnant" woman. Tonight, they are on the lookout for two specific runaways, one fourteen and the other sixteen years old. This time they have pictures of them—they are both blond and attractive. The pictures show them in affluent surroundings. The officers stop two girls, but they are the wrong ones. We go into the Port Authority police office and they explain that they have two phone numbers as leads—that's all! The Port Authority police try the numbers. They trace one to a Queens phone booth. The other number was one given them by the girls' parents as a place where she may possibly be reached. That one turns out to be the home of one of the girls' friends. Since the Port Authority police can't leave the premises, they feel a little helpless. They have already tried both numbers and received very little information.

They suggest that I call the friend, disguising myself as "Candy," a fellow runaway. When I do, a girl answers and identifies herself as Dee. I tell her that Susan, one of the runaways, told me to call there, that Dee knows where the other girls can be found. For a moment she seems to be going for the story. She answers nervously, saying that she does not know where they are. She claims that she has not seen them. From the confusion in her voice and the whispering in the background, we conclude that she may know something; the girls may even be there.

After I hang up, the officers decide that we should go out to Dee's house in Queens. We get the address in Queens, but not the apartment number. None of us knows his way around in Queens very well, but after some searching and with a few good guesses, we find the house. It turns out to be in a nice middle-class neighborhood. It seems an unlikely place for a runaway to hide. Inside, we find the name on a mailbox and proceed to the apartment. The officers place me in front of them, so that when the people open the door, they won't see the two policemen first and possibly slam the door. Instead, they'll see a small woman in jeans, looking harmless. A voice from the inside asks, "Who is it?" "Me," I answer. The door opens.

Dee, who is fifteen, is sitting there with her parents and acting very nervous, daring to say nothing. She claims not to have heard from the two girls since morning. She says she has seen nothing and knows nothing. It is clear that she isn't going to say anything in front of her parents. Her parents act annoyed, as if they have had enough of this drama. They promise to contact the runaway unit should they hear of anything, and politely invite us to leave. Dee looks worried about the girls, one of whom is her best friend. She seems to want to say something but doesn't.

At that we give up and start on a long, gloomy ride back to Manhattan. It is getting late and we are getting hungry. It has been a futile evening. First, a search for a girl on Delancey

19

Street, what we thought would be a sure shot—full identification, everything. Everything, that is, but the live body. An hour or so spent getting gas. At least two hours going to Queens and back, for two girls who weren't there. No new leads, no information. We return to Port Authority to give the sad news to the parents who have come from New Jersey to look for their daughters. Since we haven't found them, they decide to go out and look for them themselves.

Starved, we plop down at a hamburger restaurant. It's close to 10:00 P.M. We are eating fast and staring out the window at the same time. These two men can't even eat a hamburger without watching, their eyes constantly searching. One of the officers notices two young girls. The girls seem to be street-walking. Are they runaways? Or are they sixteen years old? Are they "cruising," or just looking for their dates. Maybe they are only out taking a walk.

The girls disappear. Then they turn up again. We hurriedly finish our meal. One of the officers runs out just as one of the girls is driven off in a car. The other has disappeared again too. In search of the girl who didn't get in the car, we walk around the known hotels, searching among rows of painted girls leaning against the walls. We wait a good while. No sign of either of them. We leave and walk back to the Times Square area.

Now we are looking for the two girls we didn't find in Queens—or any other runaway. I see a very young-looking girl dash out of a topless bar. She is dressed in pink hot-pants and getting into a cab. I feel sure of success. I point her out to the men, thinking I may get a police medal for this someday. Officer McGinniss, who is driving, looks into the rear-view mirror and spots her. They know her. They've picked her up before and know she's seventeen. They tell me something of her situation. Her mother is in jail and the girl ran away from her aunt's house. The aunt, who has children of her own, felt she could no longer handle the girl and did not want her to come back. So at seventeen, she roams about the bars, the

20

hotels, and topless joints, and most of the time stays half drunk.

It is getting late, and we are tired. Knowing that so many kids are out there and unable to find even one to return home, we feel sad, a bit frustrated.

We return to the spot near the hamburger restaurant where we saw the two girls. As we walk along, Sergeant Greenlay says to me, "In order to run this unit properly, I'd need a staff of twelve or fifteen, so that we could be out here seven days a week. You really need to be able to stay out here and just watch them before you can do anything."

Just as he finishes speaking, we look up and see Officer McGinniss across the street talking to one of the girls that we saw from the restaurant. We cross the street to them. The man she has just picked up is waiting in case she is let go. Officer McGinniss is not satisfied with the identification. It seems she uses two different names and it isn't clear which one is really hers. He politely asks her if she'd mind coming down with us to verify the information. She's a bit frightened and says, "Not at all." She tells us to call her Maryann.

She's a nice-looking girl, claims to be twenty-one years old but looks much younger. We soon learn that she arrived in New York only within the last twenty-four hours. We get into the car, she and I in the back. She offers me a cigarette, as if we'd been friends for years. Then she starts asking questions about what kind of neighborhood it is that we are driving through. She asks the officers if they'll be returning her to her original spot since she'd have trouble finding her way back. "Sure," they answer. "We hope you don't mind being inconvenienced."

We go a few more blocks and suddenly Officer McGinniss slams on the brakes. Sergeant Greenlay dashes out even before the car completely stops and approaches a girl who looks like the girl we saw with Maryann earlier. And sure enough, it's the right girl. What luck, finding both within a few minutes' time. That doesn't happen too often. Melody looks even younger than Maryann, about fourteen or fifteen. Sergeant Greenlay asks her to get into the car. Much more hesitant than Maryann was, she wants to know what this is all about —after all, she wasn't even picking up a man, she was just on her way home.

As we start driving down to the office on Twelfth, Melody takes out a very solid-looking piece of identification that states she is eighteen years old. That would make her as legal as she can get. We call her folks in Kansas, but they are not home. We talk to her brother, who is thirteen, and her sister who is nine. They both say they know their sister is in New York. They tell the officer that Melody graduated from high school last year and therefore should be eighteen. It now looks as if she's too old to be a runaway.

Before taking her home, we get to talk to her. She tells me that there are seven girls she knows who are here from Kansas. They all used to work a bar in Kansas and then came to New York and are all working as prostitutes. As is usual among prostitutes, she won't tell us a thing about her pimp or the operation, how the girls from Kansas all got here or what place they work out of. However, in the course of her rapid talking and giggling, she shows us a picture of her roommate, who turns out to be a girl the officers were looking for the week before—a runaway. Saying nothing to her, they take down all the information. That will be tomorrow's task.

Melody tells us that the man she works for is saving all her money. When she stops working, which is supposed to be this Christmas—about seven months away—she's going home. She plans to buy a house, get a car, maybe get married and eventually have kids. I ask her why she doesn't save her own money, why she needs to have her pimp do that. She just shrugs and doesn't answer. She talks a lot about all the money she has made, but she has only five dollars with her tonight. She mentions in passing that she has never seen the passbook of her "savings account," the one in which all her hopes for the future seem to be placed. It's hard for us to believe how naive

22

she is. We are all thinking how tragic it will be for her when she learns she's been fooled all these months.

At the time, no one seemed satisfied about the phone call to Kansas. Even so, after talking to her for a while, we no longer think she is a runaway. She seems almost pleased that her work was interrupted.

Maryann was identified by her mother, who lives in Minnesota, as being almost twenty years old.

Well, it's way past midnight. We return both girls to where we found them. After dropping off Maryann, Officer McGinniss turns and says, "We really do have some good nights. Tonight just wasn't one of them."

In hopes of witnessing a more successful evening, I went out once again with the runaway unit. That night, on our way to getting gas for the car, the officers picked up Patty B., just as she was going into a Lexington Avenue hotel. It turned out that this was the fifth time they had picked her up and they all knew each other well. Patty was a sixteen-year-old, with an extensive history of heroin addiction. She seemed to be a symbol of the lost generation, of all the kids who have no place to go. She had been in trouble of one kind or other for years—ever since her mother had remarried. At thirteen, she had started coming home late. By the time she was fourteen, she had gotten into heavy drug use. Now, at sixteen, she was no longer using heroin, "just" cocaine and marijuana, but she'd become a prostitute.

This time she had run away from an "open door" training school for girls in Trenton, New Jersey. Officer McGinniss would have to call her mother and let her know that Patty had been found again in New York. But before calling the mother, we took some time to talk to Patty. Knowing full well that the last thing Patty wanted was to go home, Officer McGinniss suggested to her that she go into a "locked" drug-treatment program, that is, one in which she is confined and cannot sign herself out. She said she thought her life was perfectly all right, living with a man here in New York, no longer shooting up with heroin. But with a lot of persuasion, she was fairly well convinced that going into a program would be better than going home. The talk had taken a good hour.

It was arranged that Officer McGinniss would present the plan to Patty's mother. As he made the call, Patty, who was chain-smoking and biting her nails, stated matter-of-factly, "She ain't gonna go for it. You'll see, she'll make me go home or have me put in jail." When the call was finally made, Patty's mother was not at home, though she'd be back soon. Patty smiled as if she'd won a major battle. Obviously smart, a real manipulator, she seized the time to start asking Officer McGinniss about the "locked" drug-treatment program. She suggested that he start making arrangements right away, before her mother got back. Officer McGinniss was almost falling for it, but he didn't have the authority to make those arrangements. Patty showed us her arms, saying, "Look, I ain't got any new marks." Sergeant Greenlay looked pleased. By that time, all of us had spent a good part of the evening sipping coffee and talking with Patty, and seemed to have become her friends.

Just then the phone rang and it was the mother. Patty couldn't have been more right. Her mother certainly did want her back. But, that wasn't the only problem facing Patty. As it turned out, the issue was not only between Patty and her mother, but also between Patty and the New Jersey authorities. We hadn't known until then that there were several criminal charges against her. At the time she had run away, she was supposed to have been at home, having been released by the court into her mother's custody until she was twenty-one. Since her mother had reported her missing, this was a violation of parole. The New Jersey authorities wanted her back. They wouldn't consider the idea of a locked drug-treatment program. They did not trust Patty to stay anywhere very long. They insisted on our returning her the very next morning.

It was only 9:00 P.M. So the task at hand was to put Patty

into a locked facility in New York for the night. The only locked facility for juveniles is Spofford.

By that time, no one was enjoying the evening anymore. Patty was protesting vehemently, becoming hysterical, getting ready to cry. "They are going to lock me up. Why did you do this to me?" she demanded. Her only hope at that point was to find a way to get away from us—the act of disappearing that she's so good at. While the arrangements were made for Spofford to take her in for the night, Patty went into action.

First, it was the bathroom scene. She must have gone to the bathroom five times. Then, she decided she was hungry. After all, she'd been there since six o'clock and now it was almost ten. The idea that the officers might just be dumb enough to let her go get something to eat was apparently a bright spot in her life. But Sergeant Greenlay asked her what she wanted to eat and went out himself for it.

When it became apparent to her that she was really being sent back to New Jersey, Patty made a call to "T" to tell Joe in the hotel to pick up her stuff. The man on the other end understood clearly what had happened to Patty. "Looks like you won't be working tonight?" was all he said. Patty just answered "No" and hung up.

Sitting down quietly to eat her all-American meal, she happened to face the bulletin board full of pictures of runaways. There were smiling pictures, school pictures, most of them of fourteen or fifteen year olds. Her eyes were glued to those pictures, methodically going down the list: K.G., 13, 114 pounds, missing since 1974, last seen in the company of a male; M. Smith, 16, missing since 1975, last seen wearing blue jeans and a sweater leaving for school. There were some thirty pictures tacked on the board. Many of them were gray and dusty, looking as if they had been there for a long time. Underneath some of the photos was a short note: *Arrested,* or *Found dead,* or *Returned home.*

McGinniss tried to tell her that, when they face the judge,

she should scream and holler. That way, maybe they won't lock her up, but instead send her to a drug facility. While all the arrangements were being made, Patty decided to tell me that three days earlier she had been arrested in New York for robbery, and released. She had given them a phoney name, so she thinks they won't find her. These new developments didn't faze the men. Officer McGinniss was getting ready to transfer her to Spofford, while her mother was supposed to make arrangements for her in New Jersey.

At 10:00 P.M., as instructed, her mother called back. When Officer McGinniss finished his dealings with the mother, he handed the phone to Patty, who until then had not said a word to her folks. She smiled instinctively as she started talking to her mother. They started trying to convince her mother that she needed to go into the hospital. She pulled up her sleeves exposing some very ugly, slightly infected bruises. She told her mother that she had eighteen stitches on her arms from some mysterious accident. Apparently getting a little sympathy from her mother, she asked about her sister, her brother, her cousin, and, it seemed, anyone else she could think of. Getting settled into a friendly conversation, she became much calmer. Then her sister got on the phone. They got into a long conversation on all sorts of subjects, from what she'd been doing for the last three months, to the weather in New York. She ended by putting all the blame on the mother: "You know why I can't go home . . ." Just about then, Officer McGinniss, who had been filling out endless reports, decided that the phone call had gone on long enough. "Now, say good-bye. You'll see them tomorrow."

With all her earlier attempts to get away frustrated, she decided she wanted to go to a hospital to have her arms taken care of before going to Spofford. "Spofford has a nurse. She'll take care of it," said McGinniss. By this time all of us were starved and really tired. At eleven o'clock, we were still waiting for a call from New Jersey. We had to get what they call the missing persons alarm number before they'd accept her in

26

Spofford. The New Jersey police had been looking for the number for some three hours. Patty should only know we'd been holding her illegally all this time, since no warrant number or missing person's alarm number had been supplied.

While we were waiting for the New Jersey police to call, she started to read an article in the paper. It was the article on Karen Baxter, the young runaway who was working as a prostitute and killed in a Lexington Avenue Hotel. "I used to work there," Patty said. I asked her if she had known Karen. She said, "Yes. You know, room 202 used to be my run."

Around midnight, the call finally came and we all drove up to Spofford. The facility is in the Bronx. The borough was as lively as it is during the day. Bongos were playing, people were singing, all in the midst of many signs of poverty, falling down buildings, garbage. Finally we reach Spofford. Officer Mc-Ginniss hurried in with Patty before she could run away. In two minutes he was back out with her. "You won't believe this," he said, "but the nurse wants us to take her to Lincoln Hospital to have her arm looked at." And then with fatigue in his voice, "That's an all-night production."

The emergency room at Lincoln Hospital looked like Times Square. There must have been a hundred people waiting to be treated, even at 12:30 at night. There were gun-shot wounds, stabbings, all kinds of diseases that poverty brings on. There we were with Patty who had a bruise on her arm. The policeman on duty took a look at the two tired officers and in no time at all a doctor appeared. He bandaged her arm and said a friendly good-bye. As we left, some of the poor sick people were yelling at us for getting ahead.

Patty had really thought this time she'd get away. She had been hoping to be hospitalized, knowing the city would not assign a police officer just to baby-sit for her. Back to Spofford. As Patty kissed me good-bye, she said, "I'll see you all next week." And most probably she would.

Is it worth it all? Well, there are maybe a million kids who run away from home each year, some say as many as two mil-

lion. The runaway unit in 1976 found and returned or otherwise serviced a few more than three hundred kids. That's a
small number (particularly small that year since for six
months of it there were only two officers on staff). But the
officers think that returning even one runaway is worth their
effort. "We have to care about our future," says Officer
McGinniss.

The Runaway Center

Not all runaways go home. Some can't—there's no home to go to or their parents won't take them back. Many others shouldn't go home. For instance, a social worker told me about one particular case, "That kid is the only sane member of her family—and that is because she ran away from it. She did the very best thing that she could do, leave." Home is far from the best place for some kids—home is where the child is regularly beaten or psychologically abused, where an alcoholic parent makes a hell of the home, where fierce fights take place nightly.

Of course, runaways also come from good and seemingly happy homes as well. But many of those runaways end up back at home sooner or later, perhaps under the care of a counselor or a psychiatrist, receiving the help he or she needs to lead a useful life.

But where does the runaway go who comes from a home that is plagued by turmoil? Runaways in this group are most often too old for adoption but too young to be on their own without falling prey to street crime. Fortunately, there is a place for them—the runaway centers. These are places where teenagers who cannot or should not go home can live with their peers under adult supervision.

Runaway centers are as different as the kids in them. Some are small and some are large. Many of them are run and managed by the Catholic Church; others are managed by the kids themselves; some centers are only temporary shelters; others serve as permanent homes for the residents.

Project Place in Boston, Massachusetts, is one of the runaway centers I visited. It is situated on a lovely, quiet, clean, tree-lined street in a neighborhood of family homes.

I found the address at the very end of the block. A dog came from the building to greet me with loud barks. As I entered, music was blasting, and the place definitely needed a good vacuuming. Kids were relaying messages from the first floor to the third, yelling over the beat of James Brown. Some were getting ready to go swimming. One girl was going to get her physical. "You have your card for the hospital, don't you? No? Now why the hell would you go all the way to the hospital and not take your card with you?" In no time at all, the place cleared out. A few youngsters were still milling around the house: one guy was sleeping, another was painting his room a deep purple. There was lots of motion—lots of life in this house. It was almost like a teen-age social club, kids dancing and singing, yelling to each other in the latest slang. Actually, this place knew many sad stories of teenagers, many of whom have no other home but this one.

Project Place is always lively, noisy, and full of teen-age energy dispersed in what seems like adolescent chaos. Imagine a house filled with a dozen or so teenagers of both sexes. It's a little like a college dormitory, except its residents are younger—fourteen to eighteen. The kids take turns cooking, particularly the evening meal. I kept telling myself, you really have to be youthful and energetic to work here. The sheer activity of the place could drive you to exhaustion.

Except when there's a vacancy, each room is shared by two girls or two boys. All the rooms are decorated with pictures from the latest magazines, and posters. It seems ironic that a room filled with pictures of Richard Roundtree or Donny and Marie houses a girl who has seen the very worst of street life, been through the most extreme experiences, and yet her fantasies are the same as any other teenager's.

The runaway centers provide many services and fill dozens of needs. Many of them are staffed by men and women who are only in their twenties and still remember being teenagers themselves. In a way, living in a family consisting of one's peers and authority figures hardly any older is a very healthy system. The young people seem to develop strong ties with each other, learning to rely on members of their own age group rather than their biological parents, learning to be independent, and preparing for adulthood.

Some of the residents in the center go to school. Others look for work or go to a training school. Still others spend much of the day hanging out in their rooms, talking to members of the staff, answering phones, typing responses to letters that come to the house, or raiding the refrigerator.

The atmosphere at Project Place is cozy and accepting. The few staff members are obviously close to the kids. There are no directors, no titles, no last names. It's run as a collective. Staff members and residents have equal say in how things are to be run. Dirty towels, or hairbrushes out of place seem to bother no one. A curfew is set for both residents and staff members, during the week and on the weekends, but a few minutes of lateness would upset no one. Staying out all night is not unheard of, but the person is expected to call if they won't be returning to the house. Sex is not permitted in the house, but it seems to be no secret that everyone is involved with somebody in or out of the program. Advice is given freely, and if someone seems to be in an unhealthy relationship, he or she is encouraged to end it. But no threats are made, no ultimatums issued.

The counselors give the residents a long rein. They seem to act as advisers rather than their parents, at least where telling the runaways how to behave is concerned. The house has rules, but rules are broken or altered without a big to-do. Liberalism prevails, and to a large degree, the residents determine the direction of their own lives. There is some structure. There is a schedule, but it is not the center's major feature. One staff member explained their philosophy this way: "You can't treat them as if they were kids. They have been out there on their own, making it by whatever means they could. So it's silly to get all upset when someone comes home late. They have been alone on the streets for years, with no one telling them that it was time to go home. What we try to do is talk to them a lot and explain why, for their own good, they shouldn't do one thing or another. But you can't change their patterns overnight. If you tried to do that, they'd run away from this program, just like they ran away from home."

Not all the runaway centers are like Project Place. Some have a much more traditional approach to what a teenager's upbringing is all about. Many of these centers are run by the Catholic Church. And there is more concern for discipline than at, say, Project Place. One of those centers is Covenant House in New York City. It is loosely affiliated with the Church: Of eighty staff members, nine are priests or nuns. Actually, Covenant House is now nine different centers, and can house up to a hundred people. Like Project Place, the Covenant House is located in a handsome brownstone on a lovely residential block. As I walked in the door, I was greeted by Sister Mary, a pleasant nun wearing a habit. Unlike Project Place, the girls and the boys are housed in separate facilities. I was visiting the girls' part.

Some of the girls were out attending school, but others were in the house, quietly sewing, or reading. The place was very quiet and orderly. Sister Mary was clearly in charge. She cooked the meals with the help of the residents. The place was orderly, very clean and neat. There was not the dorm spirit of Project Place. Here, the staff is staff and the kids are kids. Structure and rules are considered an important part of teenage life. One of the administrators explained how their approach was acceptable to the parents and good for the kids as well: "It's hard enough to accept the fact that your kid ran away and will not come home to live for a while. At least in this place the parents can feel certain about their children's being in good hands and under close supervision. We also believe that kids need a strong hand in guidance. They need advice, and direction. We don't leave them to their own devices."

Some argue that the kids themselves prefer the discipline of a situation like Covenant. The girls are separated from the boys, and sex is clearly not a part of this center. In fact, one of the staff members put it firmly: "While they are out there, they are abused and misused sexually so much, that sex seems to be the one thing they don't need while they are getting their heads together. They had too much sexual freedom too early. Now they need someone to teach them that it's better when love goes along with sexual relationships." In short, the kids here are considered to be in trouble, and therefore in need of help.

While at Covenant, some of the residents receive training in vocational skills. Some go to school. The services of social workers are available to help the kids straighten out some of their problems. The older ones try to get a job, at least on a part-time basis. There are counselors to talk to, and every resident serves as a source of comfort to every other resident. The center provides a place to stay, regular meals, people to go to for help, and a way to stay off the streets and out of the crime world that would otherwise be their only means of survival.

Contact, another program in New York City, runs three different units for handling three kinds of cases: There are a crisis-intervention center, a short-term program, and a long-term residential program. The crisis center serves an essential need. It is a place a kid can call to receive help immediately.

33

In fact, one girl told me that she called Contact *before* she ran away, so they would reserve a bed for her. Sort of like making a hotel reservation.

The crisis center is situated in the East Village, not far from what was the center of the hippie movement in the 1960s. Contact has been in the business a long time. The staff at the center has seen the neighborhood change and the kids change somewhat. But some of the problems always stay the same. A kid calling may need a place to stay, a meal, a lot of counseling, or the impetus to change the way he or she is living—a way to get out of the streets, to make the courts, the reform schools, the juvenile shelters all a part of the past. At Contact they know that kids who have run away or who are in trouble with the law are in the same situation: They need help in getting off the streets, away from crime. They need someone to show love and care.

I went by the crisis center one afternoon. It was jam packed with kids. Some were runaways; some, the nomads of the inner city. Some were just neighborhood kids looking for kids their own age to hang out with. They were of all races. Two girls from Greenwich, Connecticut, were there talking to the director, who was arranging to call their wealthy parents. A girl who was no more than fourteen was giving directions over the phone to someone about seventeen. The radio was on. Some kids were playing a game. There was clearly no shortage of action.

The crisis center handles all kinds of calls from parents and kids, as well as from social workers trying to place a client for the night. As the director was making arrangements for the parents from Greenwich to come pick up their runaway children, another staff member was making calls to see if there was an empty bed someplace for a fifteen-year-old girl who was not yet ready to go back home.

"What happens when you have a runaway here who's not yet ready or willing to call home?" I asked.

"They have two to three days to make that decision," the

director answered. "By that time we *have* to notify the parents, even if to say no more than that the kid is alive and well. I'm a parent myself. I could never permit the kids to stay here and not call home. I have heard those parents shout with joy when I call and say, 'Your daughter is here and safe.' I know what that must feel like to a parent."

When the runaways first arrive, they are usually not yet ready for that call. Then, after a day or so, they are ready to give their parents' phone number. Most of the time, one of the staff members calls, ending a horrible period for the parents, a period when every time the phone rang their hearts beat faster. Now, finally, the phone is ringing and the voice on the other end is the one they have been waiting to hear for so very long.

"Hello, is Mrs. Jones there? Is this Mrs. Jones? How do you do? My name is Barbara, and I am calling for your daughter Cindy."

There will be screams at the other end, then hurriedly the mother asks, "Is she all right? Where is she? We'll come right away and pick her up."

"Well, she's just fine. She came into a program for runaways. If you like, you can say hello to her."

Cindy hesitates and then gets on the phone. Her voice is unsteady; she's holding back tears. "Mom, I'm fine. I am at this place. My counselor will explain it to you. I want to see you, but I'm not coming home." At that point, she quickly gives the phone back to Barbara, who patiently explains that Cindy does not want to go home, but arrangements can be made for a meeting between Cindy and her parents. When Barbara gets off the phone, Cindy looks relieved. She now seems anxious to see her parents again, but also a bit scared. "You know, they'll never go for my staying here." Barbara assures her that it will be all right, and to stop worrying. Cindy was placed in the short-term program, waiting to see what the outcome of the meeting with her parents would be.

The short-term program is also called "the crashpad," because it is often just that—a place to stop running for a week or two. The crashpad serves a number of functions. It may house a kid in need of emergency shelter for a night, or a kid may live there for several weeks before he or she is moved into a long-term facility.

The crashpad is in a neighborhood altogether different from the quiet street of the Covenant House facility I visited. The crashpad is on Fourteenth Street, which is very like the Times Square area. It is a crowded, dirty street frequented by prostitutes and addicts, some of whom are being treated at the methadone clinics nearby.

As you would expect, at Contact's long-term facility the routine is less structured and the atmosphere less formal than at Covenant House which is run by the Catholic sisters, but there is more evidence of adult supervision there than at Project Place in Boston. The program facility consists of several apartments in one house, a staff member or married couple living in one apartment, the residents of the program in the others. The couple at Contact were like surrogate parents. Every few minutes their doorbell was ringing—a resident was asking questions or needing something or other.

All the teenagers I met there seemed comfortable where they were and at peace with themselves, but no one was making plans to return home. Many of them were as old as seventeen or eighteen, and many months, even years, had gone by since they had run away from home. Most of them said their families had accepted the bitter fact that they might never again come home to live. "My folks come to visit me, and I went home for Thanksgiving dinner," one resident responded when asked about her family. According to the married couple who live with the residents, some parents call regularly to see how their kid is doing, and some residents go home to visit occasionally. In other cases, the kids and parents have nothing to do with each other.

All the youngsters were warm and friendly. They loved to

talk about why they had run away, but the running away was very much a past part of their lives. They were no longer missing persons. Their families knew where they were and most were resigned to living apart from their offspring. The kids were no longer concerned with finding a way to go home. They were concerned with how they were going to get out on their own, put together enough money for an apartment, for instance. They seemed like any normal adult who is worried about making ends met.

One girl had a boyfriend who at one time had also been in the program but who now had an apartment and was attending college in the city. She was planning to move in with him soon. Another girl, who had never liked school, was planning to get a job. One of the guys was about to graduate from high school, so his studies were about the only thing on his mind. For most of the kids, this place is the last stop on the road to full adulthood. Some were extremely bitter about how they'd grown up, being shuttled around from place to place. Others were not looking so much at the past, but rather forward to adulthood, in hopes that it would bring greater pleasure than the past.

What will happen to the kids when they leave the shelter is hard to say. Some manage to stay off the streets developing new habits and living a life marked by some degree of order. Others, who carry deeper emotional scars, have more difficulty getting along and living a healthy existence outside the center.

Each program for runaways is a little different, but each offers some essential service. In addition to the residential programs are the programs that specialize in referrals. The Boston area has an excellent program of this type. Called the Bridge Over Troubled Waters, it reaches out to the kids on the streets, referring them to the appropriate residence, usually Project Place.

Who are the kids in these programs? Although statistics are sketchy and at times misleading, a vague picture does exist of the young people who come to the runaway centers for help.

Nationwide, most of the kids in the centers are females—about 64 percent—and the average age is about 14.9. Other statistics available are only by area. Let us take Boston as an example.

Project Place reports that of the runaways who come to live there, 66 percent are Catholic, 19 percent are Protestant, and 1 or 2 percent Jewish. But here we must add that the balance of religions among the groups varies greatly with the region under study. May and June are very popular times for running away. Some suggest the report-card time is when kids often decide to run away.

The family background of most of these kids is grim. Sixty-one percent of them come from broken families. Even among the families that are intact, 29 percent of them are considered unstable, and 27 percent are viewed as uncertain. The runaway from a broken home has usually lived with the mother, a few with the father, some with relatives, others with foster parents. In almost 40 percent of the cases, the runaway is the oldest child in the family, and often comes from a household of seven or more children. When a runaway is asked the reason for running away, "a family argument" is by far the most common answer given. Parent-child conflict is considered the reason in 76 percent of the cases, the family argument apparently being a manifestation of a long-term conflict, at least from the child's point of view. In 15 percent of the cases, "personal problems" is given as the reason—very often pregnancy is the "personal problem," or drug use. About 7 percent of the runaways at Project Place were classified as having a major problem with drug use. Forty-three percent smoke marijuana and about 25 percent drink alcoholic beverages regularly. Most of the residents have histories of court involvement. At the time of my visit, nearly 40 percent of them were waiting court appearance.

This is the picture presented by Project Place, with its several facilities in the Boston area. The picture was similar in other areas, with the notable exception that while 77 percent of the runaways in Boston are white, with only 19 percent black and one percent Hispanic, in other areas as many as 90 percent are white; and in New York City the black and Hispanic percentages are larger.

However, two things stand out at facilities everywhere. Those are that most of the residents are female, and a disproportionate number are first-born children. Also very common is the case of a broken family, with only a mother to care for several children. One other fact common to all areas: for most of the residents, it is the second or third time they had run away from home.

At Contact, in New York, I met a very lovely girl, Susan, who had a face that personified innocence. She had only recently run away from her home in New Jersey and had not yet been touched by the street life. The officers in the runaway unit told me there was such a thing as an out-of-town look, and I began to see that look about this girl. She wore almost no makeup at all and in general lacked the sophisticated urban look. Her hair was worn parted in the middle, which seems to be the most popular of all the teen-age hair styles. Her jeans were not faded, as would be fashionable in New York. But she smoked nonstop—as if she weren't sure she'd have a chance later on in life. I asked her why she had run away.

"I just couldn't take it anymore. I was doing everything in that house. My mother couldn't deal with anything." Susan had a brother, whom she seemed to love deeply. "I hated to leave him there. I call all the time to see how he's doing." Susan's mother is a suburban housewife whose husband, though he is seldom home when anyone in the household is awake, runs the house with an iron hand. He spends a great deal of money on horseracing and on other women, according to Susan. He comes home rarely, and when he does, he spends most of his time insulting his wife and children. Unable to deal with the situation, Susan's mother had turned to tranquilizers to try to relieve her unhappiness. There was very little money around, so Susan and her mother had both taken part-time jobs. As the mother became increasingly nervous, Susan had taken on the responsibility of raising her brother. Unable to stand up to her husband, the mother's mental health disintegrated. She had become very withdrawn and was continuously depressed. Susan had left several times before, but finally, at age fifteen, she ran away for good. First she went to her boyfriend's house, but she could see that that wasn't going to work. Then she left New Jersey altogether and went to New York. Having no place to go, she called the National Hotline for Runaways and wound up at Contact. When I met her she had been there only a few days, but already acted as if this had been her home for years. She knew everybody and introduced me to everyone there like a senior resident. She was a lively teenager, acting like a teenager—something she felt she had never been before.

Another runaway, Mike left home for a very different reason. He was also the oldest—there were four children in his family—but he had very few responsibilities at home. He took out the garbage, perhaps, when his mother nagged him, and at times would wash the dishes, but that was about it. When he left home he wasn't yet sixteen.

Mike had always been big for his age. By the time he was thirteen, he had started hanging out with the fifteen-year-olds. His Saturday-night activities consisted of breaking windows, stealing cars for joy rides, harassing girls, and getting drunk. He got away with it because his father worked a second job on the weekends and Mike's mother was too afraid of him to do anything. As Mike got older, he started skipping school frequently, or, when he did go, getting sent to the principal's office regularly.

On one occasion he broke a store window and ended up in court. For that he was given a warning by the judge, a good beating by his father—and a new and higher status among his peers. After that he stayed out of trouble for about a month. By this time his marks were way down, and he couldn't have caught up if he had wanted to. He didn't want to stop spending time with the old crowd, he didn't want to change his ways. Being "bad" gave him status, he was looked up to, he was famous in school for generating fear among the students.

One of the many days that he stayed home from school, his father came home for lunch. Mike knew he'd be angry and took refuge in the closet. But as fate would have it, he moved and knocked something over which made a big noise that his father heard. Mike listened as his father got up from the lunch table, came into the other room, and opened the closet. There stood Mike. That called for a sound beating. He was also forbidden from going out at night for a month. That same day, still smarting from his beating, he got into a fight with his little brother, giving the younger boy a bloody nose. When the kid brother reported the incident to their father, who was still angry at Mike for staying home from school, not only did Mike get another beating, but a shouting match ensued which got louder and louder and uglier and uglier. Mike left home before dawn the next morning. He left, hoping that his father would be worried sick over him, but it was his mother who suffered the most. His father felt relieved, having given up on his son.

Within a few days Mike showed up at one of the runaway centers. He called his mother but wasn't about to face home. It was decided he would stay and live at the center for a while, in hopes that things could be patched up at home. But then Mike learned that the center wanted him to go to school. Rebelling even against the nonparental authority, he ran away from the center as well. He didn't want to do anything but hang out with the old crowd. The street was still in him. That was his real home.

"He's going to turn up soon," one staff member speculated, "because the kids he's with get into trouble regularly with the police. They'll pick him up, too, and this time he'll be in even more trouble than before, the law, the courts, school, you name it. Then it will be even harder to pull him out."

I was never able to learn what happened to Mike. I do know that his mother worried terribly and his father continued to show anger toward mention of his son. The staff at the center was hoping that he'd turn up there because it was probably the best place for him, at least until he was ready to give up the streets for good.

For the Susans, Mikes, and thousands of other adolescents, the runaway centers are the only salvation, whether as somewhere to stay the night before making the trip back home, or as a place that can *be* home for as long as it takes to get a better one.

Almost all centers reported that a substantial number, about 60 percent, do in fact return home; but, sadly, many others, like Mike, return to the streets instead. Some who live there refuse to do anything but sleep and wander about, and may never get their lives together at all. But for those who are ready to retire from street life, ready to start living on the legal side of life but feel they cannot do it at home, this is the place that can be the corrective force in their lives. A home away from home, at times the only home they have known, the only place where they'll listen to adult advice or take any kind of direction at all.

It's a painful thing for a parent to accept, that he or she has failed with a child, that someone else can handle him or her better than the biological mother and father. But, that is very often the case. And it's not necessarily the fault of the parents. Until recently, society was structured so that the grandparents, the cousins, and the aunts and uncles were very much a part of the family, other people to go to for advice and direction—someone objective to talk to. Now, the parent–child relationship is often isolated from the extended family, and that help and guidance in getting along in the home, in the outside world, is lost.

Often, the parents don't truly know what happened, how the child went from being a pretty good kid to a "problem child." But when the explosion occurs, what are a parent's alternatives? Is there any "right thing" to do? By the time an explosion has occurred, an outsider is usually the best person to turn to for help, because neither the parents nor the child can be objective about the situation any longer. The issues are clouded—no one is quite sure when or why the anger started in the first place.

Just as we are a society that is unable to deal with our senior citizens, we are not able to handle the problems of our young people either. In many cases of runaways, the child has been given too much freedom, really left in limbo, on the important issues, and dealt strictly with on the unimportant ones. It reminds me of what one of the officers in the runaway unit said: "When we call home and tell them we picked up their kid on Forty-second Street, we can't say to them, 'Look, she was out there prostituting.' All we say is, 'You should take the kid to the doctor as soon as possible!' Some seem to understand what we are trying to say, but some of the parents just can't accept it. They'll make a big deal about the dirty clothes the kid has on. Now, tell me, how can you be concerned about dirty clothes, when your kid was just picked up in a Forty-second-Street joint?"

The Throwaway Child: Urban Nomads

While talking with Susan in her small room at Contact, I was aware that the other bed was occupied by the very long body of someone who was fast asleep. The body didn't move during most of the conversation. I kept my voice low, for fear of waking her, but Susan assured me that her roommate was dead to the world. "She came in at about two o'clock in the morning, exhausted. She hadn't slept for days."

After about an hour or so, the long body began to stir, and I got a view of the girl it belonged to. She had an exquisite face, though her hair badly needed washing and her eyes were puffy from lack of sleep. She looked as if she needed a whole lot more sleep. The sweater she wore had been slept in before, and her black pants were shiny from wear. I suggested to Susan that we move our conversation elsewhere, but the roommate perked her head up and motioned that we should stay. She said she wanted to get up to eat, anyway. At that she got up to her full height of almost six feet up and stretched her arms, which just about reached the ceiling. At first, I wondered what she was doing here. Could she be young enough to be a runaway? She could have passed for a good nineteen. But when I asked her age she said she was only fifteen. "It was the hard life I led," she smiled, with mock drama. Diane was an urban nomad—one of those city-bred young who from the earliest years never live in anything resembling a permanent home. The crashpad is paradise compared with what an urban nomad is accustomed to. Moved from place to place, from shelter to shelter, Diane had had to be completely grown up by the time she was twelve years old.

Diane's mother was a heroin addict, her father, unknown. Her early days had been marked by a perpetual shifting from her grandmother, to her aunt down south, and back to her mother when her mother managed to stay sober for a period of time. By the time she was twelve years old, Diane had attended some ten different schools, without a whole year in any of them. Not long after she turned twelve, her grandmother, whom she loved more than anyone else, died. Diane went to live with her mother and her mother's boyfriend at the time. Her mother was never home. She'd stay away for weeks at a time. Then she was sent to jail for a few months leaving Diane with the boyfriend. The apartment had no heat most of the time, no water much of the time, and huge holes in the ceiling, exposing dirty pipes and wires. The only income was from Diane's part-time job, which she had managed to secure because of her advanced looks and height. She had liked school, but was seldom able to go; her job had to come first.

Actually, though, life was looking good to her. She liked her mother's boyfriend, whom she called her stepfather. He was soon to get his life together, and Diane, an urban nomad from birth, moved again, this time to a better place. The stepfather got a job, and a new girlfriend, and Diane stayed with them for a while. It resembled a home, a family that Diane had never had.

Then her mother came out of prison, and though she had never taken care of Diane for longer than six months at a time, she demanded that Diane move in with her, threatening a court case if the ex-boyfriend would not release her. Knowing he had no legal right to keep Diane, he reluctantly returned her to the same apartment on the grim Lower East Side from which her mother had left for prison. The mother, now a methadone patient, drank heavily, took various drugs besides the methadone, and lived most of the time in a stupor. Diane took a full-time job and stopped going to school altogether. The mother was receiving welfare payments, which she used for drinking money. Diane's life centered around her mother: taking care of her, going looking for her mother when she would disappear—sometimes for weeks at a time—bringing her home from where she'd fallen out on the street, or in a hallway or shooting gallery.

Then their apartment was condemned and the few other apartments in the building that were still occupied boarded up for good. Diane had landed at Contact's crashpad, when she had no place to stay, no money, and no one to care for her. Her mother had disappeared, leaving Diane worrying about her mother—the way in normal circumstances a mother worries about a child.

Sometimes called a throwaway child, an urban nomad doesn't run away in the traditional sense of leaving home, with a note, without a note, but they leave their surroundings just the same, often with the parents' knowledge. And, as with all kinds of runaways, to leave the insanity that exists at home is often the sanest step.

Luis was this kind of runaway. He walked away from home, but now stays only a few blocks from where his folks are living. He sees them at times on the streets or in the store, but he rarely ever goes by their house. "It only brings back bad memories," he says.

It's hard to imagine that life with his family was worse than his present life, but that's how it looks to him from his room in the basement of a tenement building—a place without windows, or heat, or much of anything a normal apartment has. This has been "his tent" for several months now. In addition, there are about a dozen places within a four-block radius where he can be found sleeping or catching a hot meal or a bath. At seventeen, Luis is already an old man, worn out from the day-to-day struggle to survive. Like a nomad, he's never too sure what life will bring, where he'll rest his head that night, where his next meal will come from. At times, he has gone many days without food. He has slept on subway cars, hallways, basements, public bathrooms. The basement that he picked out as his new "home" was the best in the neighborhood—cleaner, and in better shape than any other he could find. Plus it's free—and free of family turmoil, which is a lot more than you can say for his people's home four blocks away.

Luis's mother has seven living children; one child died at birth, another in infancy. Luis's father was last seen about ten years ago, when, without warning, he walked out and went back to Puerto Rico, never to be heard from again. His mother, resigned to his absence, found other men, who in Luis's estimation were all no good.

"She had a way of picking absolutely no-good men," says Luis. "After my father left, which by no means was a tragedy, since all he did was get drunk, come home, beat everybody up, and go to sleep, she found another man who treated us like crap. He took over, bossed everybody around, and beat us all the time. But my mother needed him. At least he brought some money into the house. To make a long story short, my mom got pregnant, and as she reached her seventh month, he split, leaving her, the baby, and us. Some of us went to school, one of my sisters worked part-time, and some of us turned to the streets."

The street life, the crimes, the perpetual anguish took its toll on Luis's mother. She aged early, became sickly, and began to feel out of control of her life. She found her whole existence revolving around the family courts, the reform schools, the welfare office, the hospitals. Her children were continually in trouble with the law and so she decided to place some of them into foster homes.

By this time, Luis had spent some time in a reform school for boys, where he had picked up new tricks and new friends schooled in street life and crime. Luis never really went back home. He left school in the sixth grade. His mother had remarried, taking on a few more children to try to raise in their three-room apartment. Luis was no longer welcome at home because he'd meant trouble for too many years. His stepfather blamed many of the family's problems on Luis's troubles with the law. Luis visits his mother from time to time, but she is convinced that the devil has taken over his body and that his soul is no good. One sister he was close to is on drugs and he avoids her completely because she's always begging for money. The other sister is married and has children of her own. He visits her sometimes, too, going over for a meal, but that's about all. The rest of the kids are scattered around. One's in jail, one's in the air force, some are still at home with their mother.

Luis referred to his basement as a kind of loft. It is a large, open space, and has an old sofa that had been thrown out down the block. He has a crate for a table, a few broken-down chairs, and a record player. He has two pairs of jeans, a few pairs of platform shoes, and then his radio and record player. "I couldn't live without music," he told me. He plans to make some new investments as soon as his life turns a bit brighter.

Luis is a street hustler. He does anything and everything, including some legitimate part-time work in the neighborhood. The uncertainty is a way of life, the only one he's ever known. He likes movement, action, and the mysteries that night life offers. He sleeps much of the day, going out on the streets at night, except the many nights that his basement is a place of entertainment, for this basement is really a community space. Many of the teenagers in the neighborhood are just like Luis. They come from the very same kind of life, have known the same cold realities that life in poverty brings. The basement serves a dozen or so kids, who stay here one night or two or three, and then move on to another basement for another few days. They travel light.

They have a regular network of spaces they occupy, sort of hold territorial rights to. This little urban nomadic tribe has its own membership, males and females, and keeps out strangers. From time to time war is declared. It could be a conflict over who may occupy a basement, or it could be when a member of another gang insults one of their members.

They disperse for part of the day, each doing something to bring in food, money, or some item, found or stolen, which could be converted into money. They survive more or less as a group, banking on the possibility that someone will have a good day and bring in some cash or food. In true nomadic fashion, they store nothing. If they had a sum of money, it would last no longer than if they had half that amount. It would just mean that they could buy better pot, more liquor, or some clothes. Money, they figure, was meant to be spent, and having it is a good time to celebrate. What else is money for? They survive as a group for a few months, then inevitably something happens. One leaves and moves on, they have a fight, a girl gets pregnant, relationships break up, or someone gets busted. Luis considered this basement more or less his space, though he shared it with his friends and members of his group. He moved around a little less than some of the others, who considered it essential that they stay hard to find. They were the ones who were hiding from the police, their girlfriends, a member of another gang, or someone they owed money.

Luis had had a girlfriend, a member of his group, but she had left him because she wanted to get married and settle down—at only fifteen; she'd been pretty much on her own since she was eleven. "Man, she was in a dream world," Luis said. "She was dreaming about having a house and all that."

Luis doesn't know if he'll ever have a real job. He has never even known anyone who worked regularly, nine to five.

He has no skills that could get him a job, and feels so remote from school, he'll probably never go back. The last time he read a book was five years ago. Now he reads newspapers that have been left on the subway. "You know, it's really crazy. Even if you want to get out of this life, you can't. In order to go into a training program, you have to have a high school diploma or the equivalency. In order to get either of those, I would have to go back to school for years. I don't even remember the last time I went to school. I can't spell, or write too well. Now, suppose all that school and training took five years. What am I supposed to do until then? Besides, all that don't even mean that I'd necessarily get a job. All that means is that I got a piece of paper."

Actually, whatever the realities about the job situation, Luis didn't seem to aspire to living better. His basement seemed at least as comfortable as most apartments he'd seen —plus, he had no rent to pay. In spite of the many rough times, he did enjoy himself. Some days he stayed high on pot, drank a little, but he always stayed away from heroin, and junkies. He couldn't bear it when someone told him what to do, so thoughts of working for someone else were most unpleasant. He is great at fixing things, and thinks he might like to work as the superintendent of a building. In fixing up his basement, he did some painting, a job he enjoyed. The only real fear he has is going to jail, a possibility he systematically avoids thinking about.

What is so striking about Luis is that he doesn't find his life to be strange or unique. He has kind of assumed that the way he was living was normal. He knows a lot of kids who've been in reform school and lived on the streets on their own. He has difficulty conceiving of someone who would still be at home living with his parents at age seventeen. He has never known anyone who always has heat and hot water, or has never received welfare checks. Every kid he knows grew up on the streets, risked going to jail, belonged to some gang. He has never thought his life would be different anywhere else, though on the depressing days he thinks about going to Puerto Rico or California to live, though he has never been to either of those places. "Man, it's the winter that gets me. That cold bothers me the most." But he never thinks about leaving for more than a day or two. The four city blocks where he moves around are really his home, the place he feels safe and comfortable. He has never taken on a project that required lengthy planning. The object of his game is to survive, from day to day, and not get caught at his crimes.

Luis's life is marked with uncertainty. When we first met, he had lost one part-time job working in one of the local shops, a job he held from time to time because he got along with the shop owner. It gave him a little cash that he could count on. As the weather got warmer he had been cheered up and had gotten another part-time job in the bicycle store—his favorite job of all. He loved fancy ten-speed bikes, enjoyed taking them apart and fixing them. Now that he was seventeen, he was increasingly aware that crime would come with heavier and heavier dues to pay. Prison scared him, though he knew a lot of guys who were there, so he would not be a stranger. He knew that at fifteen he might have been sent to a reformatory, or let off altogether, while at eighteen, he might have to serve a prison sentence for the same crime. He figured that his little job at the bike shop might work into a full-time position, at least as long as the bike craze prevailed in the city. If only he could figure out what to do with the winter months, he could ease out of the other professions, though he'll never give up his squatter's rights on the basement. Nor would he reduce the time he spends on the streets.

Summing up his teen-age years so far, he felt that, all things considered, he had not done badly at all. He figured that he had spent at least two of the years in reformatories though not all in one stretch, and a few months in Spofford. He had killed no one, though he had almost stabbed a person once. He had broken many windows and stolen a lot of property that belonged to other people. He had been a part of gang fights in which the blood had flowed freely, but no one had died. He isn't an addict, though he smokes marijuana regularly, takes a few pills, and consumes a considerable amount of alcohol—beer is his favorite, a six-pack disappears magically in one night.

He thinks he has one child, but he's not sure. A while back, maybe two years ago, a girlfriend of his got pregnant, then disappeared, probably to Puerto Rico. He wasn't certain whether or not she had gotten an abortion, or even if he was the father. "One thing about me that's really different is my feelings about kids. A lot of the guys in my group want to get their old-ladies pregnant. It's that machismo thing. Being a man and all. I love kids, but I don't want any—at least not for maybe ten years. Most of the girls around here have a kid by the time they're sixteen. I think that's really crazy. I tell any chick I'm with, like don't get pregnant. Make sure you're protected, because that ain't my thing. You know, some of these girls wanna hold on to you like that."

Luis's views on pregnancy, however, did not seem to limit his sex life. Every time I saw him he was with one girl or another. He introduced me to one friend as if she were a long-time girlfriend, but it turned out he had known her for only two weeks.

Overall, this was Luis's best year of the past five. He had had no court cases, no arrests, no trouble with the police—not even for shoplifting—and had seen no judges. "You know, that's a real great feeling," he commented.

In a way, the urban nomads are runaways, too. Often they are escaping from poverty, abuse, neglect, hunger, or drug-addicted or alcoholic parents. Some ran away to relieve their families of the burden of feeding them. They run to the abandoned buildings, the basements, the streets, and many of them find their new life to be better than living in the home they had known. These kids run to the streets, not in search of freedom, or a fantasy world—they know better than that

—but from the destruction that their homes represent. The urban nomads and runaways are similar in many ways, but there are differences, too.

Susan and Diane shared a room in a runaway shelter. Susan was white, an out-of-towner from a lower-middle-class background. She had run away taking only a duffle bag and her purse. Her disappearance had created a mystery at home, and some worry. Diane ran away from the subhuman conditions that her methadone-addicted and alcoholic mother created. Looking at the two girls, I thought about the differences between them. The most obvious difference was, of course, that Susan could pick up the phone, call her mother, and be home before nightfall. Diane couldn't. Luis couldn't either. The urban nomads—the children of the deformed urban life, filled with misery, poverty, and depression—have no place to go, except to wander about from basement to basement, among the abandoned buildings, in subways and hallways. The only other place for them is a runaway center or group home.

The urban nomads and the runaways from middle America have arrived at the same destination. They are both trying to survive. Diane and Susan met at the center, but they could have met on Forty-second Street, picking up a man, or in a massage parlor, or acting in a homosexual porno film. When they met they identified with each other, minimizing their differences. Diane said she may be a little better off because she looked older and could get a job more easily. Diane never stood on the corner and sold her body, a fate that seemed more likely for Susan because she knew no one in New York. Her youthful-looking face could bring in money for a pimp, a situation she had already explored. Once when Susan left the room, Diane said, "She could really be swallowed up by some dude. She's so small and cute. I'm a lot tougher, bigger and much slicker. I know what's out there. They can't play the same games with me. You know, when you're in a place like this together, you see that we are all in the same mess together. Now, it's true that a lot of these kids run away from home looking for adventure and excitement, but that wears off real fast. Then the only thing left is survival, man, by whatever means you can find."

In a way, Diane's insight was quite right. Any adventure or excitement the kids may be looking for ends quickly. Either they go home after a day or two before the dream turns into a nightmare, or they turn to the streets to survive—which provide excitement, but hardly the kind the runaway was looking for. For the out-of-town teenager, prostitution, male or female, is the quickest way to make a dollar. The urban nomad might have to stand on the corner at some time too, but a kid who grew up on the streets is more likely to have other survival skills as well. They can shoplift, steal, mug, or get a little credit from the neighborhood stores. Even more significant, perhaps, than those skills is the protection that some of the gangs offer. While many of the gangs are known for being quick with the knife, for declaring wars, and making vicious attacks, they also provide protection and assistance for some of the new members—a place to sleep, some of their food, even their drugs. While some gangs are noted for their brutality to teen-age girls, some of them protect them from prostitution and becoming prey to a man.

I was talking to Sister Lorraine Reilley, the director of GLIE—Group Live In Experience—situated near the South Bronx, an area famous for its crime and decay. Sister Lorraine (or just "Lorraine") has known plenty of these troubled kids and heard many tragic stories. "You know," she said, "America has never learned to solve its problems, only to run away from them. Like the rest of society, the kids run away from them too." GLIE serves the urban nomads, many of whom come from the gangs, the burned-out buildings, or the courts. Unlike the other centers, where the more famous interstate runaways tend to end up, most of the kids at GLIE come from the neighborhood. Many of the kids haven't been to school for years. Most are victims of neglect and child abuse.

As we were talking, a young man interrupted us. I wasn't sure whether he was a youthful-looking staff member or a mature-looking resident. "I'm going out to look for Sharon," he told Sister Lorraine, who, incidentally, dresses in street clothes and wears nothing to indicate that she represents the Catholic Church.

I wondered why the young man was looking for Sharon. The director must have picked up my unvoiced question and, sitting back, preparing for a long story, began to explain.

"Sharon is a resident who ran away from the program. When someone leaves this program, I look at the staff, not the participant. They knew what kind of background Sharon came from. I blame them for her leaving and they'd better find her. You know, when a staff member loses too many cases, I fire them. I know that they're not doing their job."

Sharon was orphaned at nine months. Her aunt took her in when she was three years old and kept her until she was nine, when she was taken away and placed in an institution. Six years later, the aunt was taken to court. It had taken them all that time to figure out they had a case of child abuse on their hands. After the institution came a foster home where the parents collected the money for her care, but spent it on everything but Sharon. It was a real hustle for the foster parents. It makes you wonder who investigates the prospective foster homes. Sharon ran away from her foster parents, who let months go by before reporting her missing so that the support payments would not stop.

After running away, Sharon stayed first with some people in the same building that she'd been living in. After six weeks, she began moving from place to place in the same neighborhood. When she had become exhausted from moving around so much, a friend suggested that she check out GLIE.

"She ran away from here because she couldn't take the rules. But you have to be flexible with the rules. You are dealing with someone whose life never had any structure, who never had any guidance in all her nearly fifteen years. You can't just clamp down on kids like that. You have to talk to them for a long time, so they can understand what it is that you are trying to say."

All the kids at GLIE have to go to school, either the school they had attended, if sporadically, before coming to live there, or one the GLIE staff feels is more appropriate. Rather than create special conditions for the kids, they try to help the kids learn to deal with the "real" world, which is where in the end they'll have to live. Most of the kids are prepared for eventually returning home, and while home may not be perfect, GLIE's conception is a holistic one. They work with the family as well as the kids. If the family needs to be relocated, they try to work it out. Individual and group therapy are offered to all the families as well as the kids in the program.

"Rather than letting them run away from a situation that may not be ideal," the director says, "we work on getting the kids and the families to work out their differences so that the kid can go back home. Some go back after a few weeks; others may take eight or nine months." GLIE is really trying to serve the total community, not just the runaways. Sister Lorraine commented, "Every four miles or so throughout the city there should be a community center to help with the community's problems."

When you consider that there are an estimated fifteen thousand children in the Bronx who are urban nomads, and the Bronx is only one of five boroughs of the city, you can figure that there may be sixty thousand, even seventy thousand, of these kids in New York City alone. When we consider this figure, then add the one million runaways, the teenagers on drugs or alcohol, the child-abuse cases, the children who grew up in institutions or reformatories, those who have committed crimes, the mentally disturbed children, and many other troubled youngsters, it's clear that some part of society's fabric has disintegrated. We are therefore obliged to examine that society to determine what is missing, what needs repair, in order to really find solutions to the problems that cause runaways and urban nomads. It's no longer a fairy tale, no longer a Huckleberry Finn adventure. This situation is real.

· 5 ·

The Parents

When we think of children running away from home, those stories come to mind of mean, terrible stepmothers tying up innocent children, working them like slaves, denying them any pleasure, so the kid ran away—and we don't wonder why. We know who's the good guy and who's the bad guy. But those are fairy tales. The parents of true-to-life runaways are as different from one another as the children are, as the situations they ran away from are. Many of the kids we are looking at are indeed running away from, say, a mean stepmother who has abused and mistreated them. And many are running away from perfectly lovely, caring families where love and attention is very much a part of the children's daily lives.

Some parents told me that they no longer concerned themselves about their children's behavior because they had attempted unsuccessfully for too many years to change it. Many of them felt that they had tried everything—the priest, the school counselor, the psychiatrist—all to no avail. Now they just prayed to God that their son or daughter would someday turn around, and grow up at last to become a mature, reasonable human being. But for now they had given up hope. They felt betrayed by their own children. They resented the lack of gratitude shown for all their efforts: "How could they do this to me?"

One morning, it couldn't have been noon, the police—members of the regular force not the runaway unit, picked up a fourteen-year-old girl for prostitution. It was the third time for her. Instead of fingerprinting her or putting her in jail, a concerned police officer took the time to talk to her. Maybe that day she looked especially pitiful. She was obviously dead tired, nearly falling asleep on the street. Dressed in a see-through blouse and jeans, she had no money, not even a purse, and her lovely face was framed by uncombed hair. She said she wanted to go home to her mother in Washington, D.C. She had a few marks on her arms that looked like somebody had beaten her up. Where she'd put her clothes, her money, and her purse, she wouldn't say. The police took her to the bus terminal, turned her over to the Port Authority police, wished her well, and hoped she wouldn't be back the same night with her beautiful brown sleepy eyes.

The Port Authority police in turn called the runaway unit of the New York Police Department for help. When the unit got there—and I was along—the girl Valerie was fast asleep on a board that only someone in need of sleep could imagine to be a bed. She woke up about as unpleasant as most of us are when awakened to face a situation we've been dreading. She gave us a phone number for her mother, which turned out to be that of the Library of Congress, where her mother did indeed work. While the police were busy calling the mother and making arrangements for Greyhound to take Valerie home for free, I bought her a Coke and took her outside to talk. We got into a police car, and she just wanted to sleep. She wouldn't tell me why she had run away, or why she had decided to go back home, but she did tell me that this was not the first time she had run away and definitely not the first time she had been in trouble with the law.

Her mother was there to receive the call, but at first only

whispered into the phone, "I can't talk here. I'll have to call you back in a few minutes." She did call back some fifteen minutes later, explaining that she didn't want to expose the situation at work. When she heard that her daughter had been found and would be returning home that same afternoon, there was no shout for joy, none of the urgent questions about her daughter's welfare. She was relieved the girl had not been found dead, and was not in a hospital, but the response was one of confusion. And when told to pick her up at the bus station, she protested, saying she would have to get off early from work, and couldn't the girl come on a later bus. The police argued that the girl would be at the bus station with no one to watch her—they certainly couldn't baby-sit for her until it was convenient for the mother to pick her up—but they had to make sure that she was at least returned safely. The mother finally agreed to pick her up and was to call once the daughter had arrived safely. Shortly, we were able to send Valerie home on the bus, but not without feeling that we'd surely be seeing her again.

Her mother's response had surprised us. She hadn't seemed nearly so happy as we'd thought she would be, having her runaway child returned. She sounded as if she'd been through the experience many times already and expected to have to go through it again in the future. She said she was tired of time and again having to pick up her daughter at bus stations. Or police stations. Or juvenile courts. Or you name it. She had been through it all.

Valerie came from a middle-class black family in Washington D.C. She had a couple of brothers and sisters. Her parents were divorced and her mother had remarried when Valerie was about ten years old. The mother held a professional position at the Library of Congress, and her step-father owned a small business. They were not wealthy, but comfortable. Ever since the mother had remarried, Valerie had been in one kind of trouble or another. She had made her parents' lives miserable, almost as if she wanted to break up her mother's marriage. Valerie admitted that though her stepfather was strict, he treated her and her siblings well.

So, why the strange behavior? No one seemed to know. Her mother had taken her to a string of psychiatrists and counselors. They had also tried family counseling. But nothing seemed to help. Her mother had learned to accept the pain and the sense of failure that Valerie's behavior caused. By this time, she was almost numb to another phone call from the New York police. There had been so many calls, so many reunions. How long can a mother grieve?

On the other hand, can a mother ever learn to live with knowing her fourteen-year-old daughter turns tricks for five dollars in rat-infested hotels? Particularly when the daughter claims to see nothing wrong with that life, that she sees no reason to go to school, to have a legitimate job. In fact, Valerie told me, in her customary blank tone, "There is nothing else that I can ever see myself being." I asked her if she thought that she could be a nurse or a secretary. "No, I don't," she answered. "I have no picture of myself as anything except what I am."

Yet, every family responds differently. While Valerie's folks resigned themselves to the unhappy state of affairs, other families don't wait for police to turn up with their son or daughter. They add their own search efforts to those of the police.

I called Mr. G. because I had heard about his daughter who had run away repeatedly from their home in a small, quiet town in New Jersey. The call was so painful, so filled with his tearful silences, his slow and deliberate fragmented sentences, I felt a little embarrassed asking the family to talk about something so painful for them. I had assumed from how emotional they all were on the subject that the situation was new to them. But I suddenly realized that they had been living with the hurt for many years. Now they were becoming desperate because their runaway daughter was soon to turn eighteen and be legally out of their reach. I had planned to visit Mr. G. in his home, but he told me that his time was limited, since he spent all his spare time searching for his daughter, sometimes with the help of one or more of his other four children. He asked if I would accompany him on his next search. I agreed.

It had been three years now since the police had first returned Mr. G.'s daughter to her home. She had been placed in a juvenile center that time, but had run away from there in a matter of days. The New Jersey authorities soon picked her up again, and this time she was returned home. Her father, afraid that she'd run away again, stayed awake all night to stand guard. But while he watched downstairs, she jumped out the window of her room on the second floor, and broke her leg. Instead of going back into the house for help, she got herself to the highway, nearly a mile from the house, hitched a ride on a truck, and managed to get back to New York. The broken leg, apparently never taken care of, healed shorter than the other, though her father, oddly, would never admit that was why.

The next time she ran away, one of her fellow runaways told on her. When she went back that time, a counselor encouraged the father to leave her alone, not to put her under surveillance. He complied with the suggestion and let her be. One night she said she was going to the store for cigarettes, and this time she never came back. It was the last time they had seen her.

Saturday morning my doorbell rang and I opened it to a man who looked older than I knew his age to be. He stood there waiting, ready for getting on with his detective job. He knew the New York streets well—the areas where prostitutes worked, the runaways' hangouts, the Bowery, Chinatown.

I got into the well-used family car, in which he carried a

map of the city and hundreds of two-by-four pictures of the missing daughter. He handed me pictures of a smiling, happy-looking teenager, about fourteen years old. On the back, in neat hand lettering, were her name, her age, her eye color, her height, her weight, and a phone number. We started out, her picture in my hand.

In all those Saturdays, some Sundays, he had not found her, but he had stumbled onto plenty of others in her same situation, prostitutes aimlessly looking for clients, for money, a free meal, a place to stay, or someone to help them break the vicious cycle they were caught in.

"Do you see that girl in the coat, the one standing there with the high heels and the coat two sizes too small for her? Once almost a year ago, I picked her up in the car when she tried to get me into a hotel. I showed her a picture of my girl. She recognized the face and told me that my daughter worked the Chinatown area. While talking to her, she let on that in a way she wanted to go home, but couldn't bring herself to call. I called her parents myself and you should have heard them scream with joy. They came to pick her up right away. Now look at her. Right back where she was."

We drove down to the Forty-second Street area, which seemed to have extended deeper into the surrounding neighborhood since I had last been there. We moved slowly, looking into doorways, on the corners, at the hotel fronts. She was not there. I wondered what her father would do if we found her and she didn't want to come with him. But on this bitter-cold winter weekend, that was no issue, for she was nowhere to be found.

Giving up in that neighborhood, we moved to the Chinatown area, where a major festival happened to be taking place. Hundreds of people were milling around the narrow streets, making it impossible for the car to move. We got out and started walking. Mr. G. was in desperation. If she was there, it would have been a miracle if we had found her. The odds were clearly against us. So was the weather. We walked up and down a few of the streets, but we were looking for a needle in a haystack.

We moved a ways back uptown into an area that during the sixties was famous for its runaway flower children, the acid freaks, and the hippies. Now the area was even more run down, and depressing-looking with burned-out tenements, boarded-up buildings, and uncollected garbage. It is still a haven for drug dealers, gangs, and runaways. Mr. G. pulled up to a building and parked the car. "That's where she used to live," he said. "The runaway unit picked her up here the last time. The apartment was listed under a man's name—her pimp." That apartment was empty now. We stayed in the car a few minutes. Mr. G. sat there looking as if he were somehow expecting her to walk out calmly any moment, but knowing full well that she hadn't been there for some time. Still, he left her picture at the local *bodega,* hoping that they just might see her one day and call. The man behind the counter pinned the picture on a wall already covered with notices of events that had taken place years ago. He said he didn't recognize the face. He wished us luck in our efforts but gave us that look that I knew too well: This bitter-cold day would bring us nothing but chill. He offered us a cup of coffee to warm us.

As the hours went by, the day grew colder, and darker. We could no longer see very well but he would not give up. To-day might just be the day she'd come out of a hotel or store, or be standing on a corner waiting for help. We passed by the hotel where the fifteen-year-old runaway, Karen Baxter, had been killed by a client of hers, a man who has never been found. Mr. G. drove by the hotel fast, then headed back to Forty-second Street, where we had started. Shortly afterward, when I left him, he was soon to be giving up the search—for the day, at least, not, by any means, for good. "If I don't find her today, I might be back next week or the week after. I'll call you when I get back. Don't forget to take her picture."

Then yelling out the window as he drove off, "If I ever find her pimp, he's dead." And I knew he carried a gun under the car seat in case he ever did.

When I had spoken to the runaway police about the case, which they knew well, having picked her up so often before, they had told me they hoped that after spending some time with the father, I'd be able to shed some light on why the daughter ran away. What was it about the home that made it intolerable to her? I did learn that Mr. G. was very conservative. A Catholic, he is, in fact, displeased with the present-day Church, because to him it is far too progressive. It wasn't hard to see that he came from the old school; overbearing discipline, even beatings, could have been a part of the family scene. He wouldn't tell me if anything in particular had happened in the past that would have made her turn against the family, and yet, none of the other children had run away. They only wished she would come back. And the father was terribly concerned, searching for her constantly, almost neurotically.

Even after getting to know the father I could only continue to wonder about what had made her repeatedly run away into the bitter cold and the filth, which, surely, no longer could represent adventure or glamour to her.

The irony glares at us—there must be some meaning in it: Why did the daughter choose to inflict on her conservative Catholic family the most severe pain that she could have—for her to become a prostitute? In their value system, nothing could be worse.

Not all parents keep up the search for their children. Some don't even want them back when they are notified that they have been picked up. They feel they have done all they could, given all there is to give. Still, they always blame themselves for the failure, wondering where they had gone wrong. And no matter how resentful of the extra hardships the parent might be, it's always dreadfully difficult to accept the loss of one's own child, to see him or her choose a runaway center, a group home, a basement, or a run-down communal apartment as home, instead of the home the parent has provided. And when the parents themselves are struggling to survive, the loss of the child may even be felt economically. A teenage working child, as long as he or she is not in school anyway, could be of great help to a family.

While many of the runaways leave home again and again, making each trip more final, others who run away return and stay. The parents of those can usually talk about the incident without the cries, the sighs, the long pauses. With less of the guilt that a runaway child always brings.

Mrs. J., one of the parents whose child came home to stay, says, "We are really lucky. We had very good counseling from the police as to what to do when our son called. We were calm. We asked him where he was calling from, but that's all. And if he wanted to come back home. When he came back, we didn't ask any questions. There was no yelling or screaming. At first he went into his room. Then we waited until he came downstairs on his own, when he felt ready to face us. Later we made arrangements with a family counselor to help us sort things out. We made some compromises and so did he."

That's a very critical time, when the phone call comes. Many parents lose their head and break down before they can even establish where the call is coming from. Then an argument develops, and before they have a chance to ask the child just to return home so they can talk the whole thing over, the kid hangs up, feeling nothing has changed—why go back there. When they do decide to return home, the arguments often take over again and the kid is gone within twenty-four hours. Only this time he'll wait longer before calling home again, if at all.

There are many kids who run away once, for a few hours, say, over an argument, a misunderstanding, or a beating. But when they run away the second time, the chances of their returning home soon are slim. And when a child runs away repeatedly, there must exist some chronic condition in the home that they are running away from. Putting a finger on what that condition is exactly, is the difficult part.

When the child leaves, it arouses tremendous guilt for many of the parents. Then if the child is not returned, does not call, continues missing, the hardship on the family increases. There are many sleepless nights, frantic calls to police, and in many cases, an increase in consumption of alcohol to try to dull the pain. The hurt goes so deep.

One of the mothers asked me, "Tell me honestly, was I wrong? All I did was try and find out where she had been until three o'clock in the morning, coming in looking high. I could smell no liquor on her breath, so I wondered what had made her act so stupid. A mother has that right, doesn't she? Don't I have a right to know?" She ended up shouting at me, as perhaps she had to her daughter, who had packed a little bag and left one night while the rest of the house slept.

Mrs. J., describing the days just after her son was returned, said, "I used to get scared every time he left the house. I used to call school every day, to make sure that he was there. If he was ten minutes late in the afternoon, I would panic. I used to have the other kids check on him. We lived in terror. For weeks, I was too scared to say no to anything he asked. Then my younger daughter started complaining that she was getting the rotten end of everything. That we didn't love her because she hadn't run away. And she had a right to complain. We really were paying more attention to the boy.

"It's been over a year now since Joe ran away, but I still can't sleep. There are nights when I wake up from nightmares. Our lives will never be the same again."

But Joe did come home to stay. He was a sensitive kid, and he particularly felt sorry for his mother. His father drank a great deal, and there were many days, according to Joe, when he didn't come home at all, or came home drunk and mean, picking a fight with anyone around. When Joe ran away and before he was found, the father came home even less, leaving his family without money for days at a time. Actually, Joe, who had never done well in school, had wanted to run away for some time. Not away from his mother or sister, but from the situation in general. But now, he felt a responsibility to fill the gap that his father's drinking had created. He was going to be sixteen soon, and planned to quit school and try to get a job. Rather heroically, really, he told me, "Running away from here now would be like turning my back on them, although I still hope to leave this place someday. It's so damn depressing. Nothing to look forward to."

Joe was like a lot of kids, his mother, like a lot of mothers, the situation is all too common: the poor, lower-class family, trying to live an honest Christian life, doing their best to pay the bills every month. Joe's dad's behavior is typical, too, ruling the house with an iron hand, beating the kids, his wife, even the dog when he comes home drunk on Friday or Saturday night; working hard during the week, putting in as much overtime as he can. The parents often argue a lot, and the kids, with their instinct for survival, stay away from home as much as possible. Joe, for instance, always hung out with the boys, getting into some teen-age activity or other. He himself drank a little, stayed out late, came home and got his beating, that is, if his father was home and awake. Joe's sister wasn't home much either, but she occupied herself being a cheerleader, baby-sitting, and reading the teen magazines. Her hopes lay not in running away, but in finding someone to marry as soon as she turned eighteen.

The families of the Joes and the Valeries on the streets, the Mr. G.'s who are still looking for their daughters in the seamy neighborhoods of New York are all in pain. Some of them are white, others Puerto Rican or black, some are poor, some middle-class. Joe has gone home, Mr. G.'s daughter is still missing. Valerie may go home but is no longer welcome. They are members of a lost generation, searching to find a way, anxiously waiting to hit the magic age of eighteen, hoping that the future will be brighter. Just as our interview was ending, one of the parents said, "It's a very hard age. They are neither children nor adults, and half of one added to half the other makes a bad combination. Honestly, they should figure out some way kids could go to sleep at thirteen and wake up when they are eighteen. Or put them all on a farm in Iowa until they grow up."

I still carry the smiling picture of Mr. G.'s daughter: C.G.; born, Oct. 5, 1958; height, 5'1"; eyes blue . . . I might just run into her and call her father. I can almost hear the shout of joy. How very happy he would be.

Runaways and Crime

When I first met Tom, he was about twenty years old. And his girlfriend could have passed for twenty-one. But Tom was just sixteen, and Margie seventeen. They both looked like adults, which is perhaps part of the runaway problem. As they say, "They don't grow them like they used to." Now a fourteen-year-old is taller than his mother, his father too, at times. It's hard to spank a kid who's a head taller than you. A child that size puts adult authority in doubt. As Tom pointed out, "When you are small, you don't feel you can answer back to them. But when you get to be fourteen and grown, they can't tell you anything. They are afraid that *you'll* beat *them* up! That's why most of the kids are able to leave, once they are bigger than and more able to stand up to their folks."

Tom, and the others in the group he hung out with, were no longer victims of the streets. They were, instead, the force that victimized, that takes advantage of the elderly, say, stealing from them what little they had. They survive predators, living off the weaker, the less fortunate, making them their prey. Tom's stories were hard to believe. He seemed such an amiable guy. He was very courteous, and anxious to be helpful to me in supplying information. It was hard to conceive that so handsome a youth, soft-spoken, and looking so nonthreatening, could have been out there on the streets, committing some of the worst crimes imaginable, making headlines in the newspapers.

"Well, I don't even know where to begin," Tom said, an introduction to a very long, at times painful story.

Tom's father was an alcoholic. He had kept Tom out of school during much of his childhood life because Tom once fell and hurt himself in school. Moreover, because of his father's bad feelings about the school environment, Tom hung out on the streets or stayed in bed and watched television. At age seven, he robbed a grocery store, taking two hundred dollars from the cash register. From then on, war was on at home.

I asked him why he had robbed the cash register.

"Well, I never had any money at home—my father would never give us any money—so I got it from there." With that, he dismissed the event almost as a natural act. As he was telling the story, he looked like a mischievous child, quite unaware of the real significance of his actions.

Tom's father terrorized the house. He threatened the family with guns. They fought endlessly, but never resolving anything. Tom left because he was afraid of being near his father, convinced that, if they continued to live in the same house, one of them would wind up dead. On one occasion, his father's drinking problem led to an incident in which the father killed somebody. Ever since that day according to Tom, his mother's mental health has been unstable. She was no longer able to deal with even simple problems and particularly not with eight children. So for a while most of the children were placed in foster homes. They had never since been reunited. At the time, Tom was trying to find his brothers and sisters, though he had little idea of where to look.

Tom himself had never been placed in a foster home. Even when some of his older brothers left home or were placed, Tom stayed on in the midst of chaos and confusion. "Beating

71

up people is what I saw all my life. Until I came into this program, I didn't even know that that's not the way to deal with things. All I knew was yelling and fighting. I have seen three people get killed in my life." One of those people was his three-year-old brother. Someone had gone berserk and accidently shot him with a gun.

The story of Tom's life was so unbelievable to me, I began to wonder whether he had exaggerated in places. So I checked with one of the counselors.

"Is everybody's father an alcoholic, which is the impression I'm getting?" I asked.

"Well, that's really not too far from the truth," was the counselor's reply. "Most of them are."

Tom ran away from the possibility of killing his father and from the insanity that his home life presented. But from violence at home, he had only come to violence on the streets. The last time he was in court had been both for robbery and for assaulting a police officer.

"Man, my record is seventy-five miles long. But that time I was really stupid. I went out with a few guys to rob a store. The police came and I hid in a Charmin's box. I didn't move. It was almost over when a policeman kicked the box, and it didn't move. He picked the box up with me in it! There was a shoot-out and one of the policeman's eyes got blown out. So I went to jail for a while and then they sent me here."

"Did you shoot the policeman?" I asked.

"No, I didn't. I can't even be sure who did. In fact, one of the other cops could have. In a shoot-out like that the bullets just fly. You can't ever be sure who shot who."

Tom's life on the streets was active, filled with being a part of the streets. He robbed people, and held up stores. He was high on something or other much of the time. He didn't stay with a gang because he felt they got in trouble too much. Also, they were too visible. He preferred doing his crimes alone. It made him harder for the police to find.

The most striking thing about Tom's manner of presenting

his stories was his seeming total lack of being sorry for his past activities. I asked him if he felt bad about anything. He answered quickly, saying that feeling bad does nothing but put people in a bad mood. Therefore, he had no intentions of feeling sad or sorry. It was part of his past, and he didn't think on it too much.

There are thousands of children in court each year for crimes committed when they were runaways. The crimes of the runaways involve not only the teenagers and their parents, but also the reform schools, the courts, the prisons, and most of all, the countless unfortunate victims of those crimes. The runaways, no matter how sad their stories, have lost much of the sympathy of the public in this way. There aren't many who will be on the side of a youth who's beating people up, robbing them, and worse.

There was a great deal of material written about runaways back in the twenties and thirties. At that time, people considered them to be mentally deranged and always the one to blame. They were viewed as juvenile delinquents. Reasons for their running away were seldom taken into consideration. Until recently, in fact, it's still the case in some places, when a runaway was picked up or returned home on his own, instead of being either sent home or allowed to stay there, he was placed in a reform school. There was a firm belief that a kid who ran away from home had to be punished. They were criminals and they had to learn their lesson. It was only recently that the tide turned, that people began to realize that maybe the kids aren't so crazy after all, that maybe the families and other causes need to be looked at too.

Now their criminal acts are forcing public sympathies away from the runaways once more. The notion of running away is again being associated with crime, reversing whatever progress may have been made. People forget that, when they left home, most of the runaways weren't involved in crime. Their street involvement is a result of having left home, not the other way around. There aren't many of them who left home so they could go out and live off the wealth of the streets. Unfortunately, the crime often becomes the only alternative to starvation. The crime of most of the runaway girls is prostitution, but some steal as well. A number of boys also survive by prostituting, but a whole range of other crimes is available to the boys. Very few kids survive on their own for any length of time working legitimately. There are very few legal jobs that a fourteen- or fifteen-year-old can get.

In 1972, juvenile court statistics revealed that more than one million juvenile delinquency cases were handled by juvenile courts in the United States. Moreover, juvenile arrests for serious crimes increased dramatically. Arrest figures for murder committed by young females showed an increase since 1960 of 215 percent and 225 percent for males. Robbery by juveniles increased 457 percent for females, 299 percent for males; burglary, 307 percent for females and 134 percent for males. We notice that the percentage figures for the most part increased much more for young females than for males, but the figures for boys were much higher to begin with. For all offenses, the percentage of increase is greater than 200 percent.

Of course, these figures are for all juvenile crimes. But it's not an accident that the increase in runaway figures and the juvenile crime figures coincide, for we know that many of the kids committing crimes are the runaways. How many of these kids are committing crimes only for food and shelter and would leave the street life if they had a place to go and someone who could put them on the right track in life? How many of these kids will spend years in jail, serving time for some horrible crime that they may have committed in their search for money? It's hard to believe that the murders we're talking about have been committed by kids who are not old enough to legally have a drink, legally obliged to go to school, and can't legally be hired to work. They are the kids in this book searching for someone who cares about them, someone who'll help them get out of the life they're in.

It's no longer the concern of only the parents to get the children back. Now, the runaways have become all our problem. How could we possibly give up on over one million youths who are our future generation? They are supposed to be our future presidents, astronauts, and doctors.

When I asked Tom what he wanted to do in his adult life, he said, "I really would like to be a veterinarian, or a drummer. I guess I'll have to settle for the second."

It is ironic that most runaways have such conventional, middle-class expectations. They rarely dream of being a great bank robber or an ace hustler. They want to go to college and be all the things valued by the middle class. Something like what their parents had wanted them to be—respected citizens, professionals.

The worst thing about the national picture are the few services that exist for the people who represent our country's future. There are eighteen states which have no centers to house runaways, not even any programs to arrange for short-term housing for runaways. Non-residential centers, where counseling and referral services are offered, exist in only fourteen states. Clearly, a lot more programs are desperately needed if this problem is to be dealt with effectively.

Perhaps even more than the residential programs and post-runaway counseling centers, we need to become involved in preventive work as well. If there were a place where a family could go for counseling long before a child gives up on his home and leaves, the acute runaway problem might quickly diminish. We need to set up family counseling centers in every neighborhood, school, and community center, where kids and parents can readily go for help and advice. We need to find a new version of the grandmother, other members of the extended family, to whom a child can turn for help. Before, children didn't have to run to the streets; they could run over to their cousins' house or their grandma's house for refuge and advice and to cool off. There was someone available to help patch up the relationship. Unless we make a serious and continuing effort to prevent the problem, we'll have to deal with over a million hopeless kids roaming the streets, sleeping on newspapers, and destroying the little bit that others may have.

It reminds me of what a runaway named Valerie said: "I don't see anything wrong with prostituting. That's the only way I know to survive." We can't afford to let a fourteen-year-old give up hope. Our country's future depends on her.

· 7 ·

Portrait of a Boy Prostitute

Joe had just arrived in New York after his short bus ride from Connecticut. He was carrying only a small overnight bag. At sixteen, his handsome face was still boyish, innocent-looking. He looked like most runaways—lost. He seemed afraid and uncertain. Most of all he looked fresh in from out of town—a look you learn to know if you have a reason to. His first stop was at a nearby lunch counter, where he ordered something to eat.

Soon after, a nice-looking man in his twenties came from across the way and sat down next to him at the counter. He struck up a conversation with the younger fellow, who soon showed signs of relaxing, his nervousness subsiding. After about twenty-five minutes the two left together.

At the back of his mind, Joe was remembering his mother's ancient warnings not to talk to or become involved with strangers. But his mother wasn't there; Joe was almost drunk on the notion that he didn't have to answer to her anymore—he could act as he chose. And he chose to go along.

Joe's newfound friend offered him a place to stay for the night. With twelve dollars in his pocket, he gladly accepted.

The friend had a studio apartment with one bed, which he said either Joe could have and he'd sleep on the floor, or they could share. Joe said they should share the bed, then no one would have to sleep on the floor. His friend seemed to go out of his way to be hospitable. He offered Joe a few drinks and a joint of marijuana. Joe accepted both. Drinking always made him feel like a grown-up, plus he wanted to impress his adult friend. He wondered if he could get away with lying about his age, but his friend seemed to be tactful enough not to ask. Joe looked comfortable with his drink—after all, he was no sissy. The marijuana was an even greater thrill—he had had the opportunity to smoke pot on only two occasions before. By the end of the evening, Joe and company were high—giggling and laughing and carrying on.

When they finally went to bed, his friend made his intentions known, and Joe offered no resistance. He was high, but even if he hadn't been, he might still have offered no resistance. He was fully aware of being a stranger in a big city, and was grateful to the person who had taken him in. In fact, he enjoyed it. And it wasn't the first time a man had touched him. He had played many games with friends, on several occasions had explored his best friend's body and always enjoyed it. The acts that this friend had performed were new to him, but not unpleasant. The next morning they woke up giggling, and stretched out in bed.

As the day got under way, Joe felt he should be moving on and figuring out what he was going to do, now that he was free from his mother. He thought about calling home, but he knew that wouldn't work. If he called, she'd want to know where he was, and demand that he return home immediately. His friend went out for a few hours and left Joe to think over what had happened. He decided that it shouldn't happen again, but he still couldn't say he hadn't enjoyed it.

Later that day, the friend came back with another friend, a boy closer to Joe's own age. He was also a runaway, so the two had plenty to talk about. Being from out of town and unschooled in the ways of this corrupt group, it never occurred to Joe to wonder why his friend had brought this other young man or how he knew him in the first place. He just thought it was a favor his friend was doing him to introduce him to a companion his own age. Joe and the other runaway, Jack, got along very well. Joe was from Connecticut and Jack from Massachusetts; both out-of-towners, both from small towns, they had a lot in common to talk about. They acted like long-lost friends finding each other in a big city by pure coincidence. Their mutual adult friend left them in the apartment, inviting them to help themselves to anything in the refrigerator.

At the time, Jack had been in New York about six months, and looked more like a New Yorker than a runaway from Massachusetts. He dressed in the latest style—blue jeans, platform shoes, and a flowery shirt. He impressed Joe. His hair was nicely groomed, on the longish side for an out-of-towner. He made a good impression. He was a quiet guy and let Joe do most of the talking. Joe told him all his troubles, trusted him with the confidential information that he was a runaway. Jack listened. In fact, Jack had heard the story many times before, but acted like a patient listener, interjecting only a few sentences from time to time about how Joe could make it in the city and not have to return home. After all, *he* is alive and well, and he didn't return home. By that night, Joe felt relaxed, and confident that he wouldn't be lonesome in the big city. Jack took him to a movie in Times Square, they stopped by a bar to have a few drinks, and Jack took Joe back to their friend's house and left him there for the night. That night he was alone in the apartment, the friend not returning till the next morning.

Joe was feeling fine about his two days in the city. He didn't miss home or school. He missed some of his pals, but not too much. He hadn't been getting along with them very well lately. He decided that the next morning he'd get up early and start looking in the paper or going around to see what kind of job he could find. He was optimistic about getting a job without too much effort. He thought he would soon get his own apartment. Then he'd call his mother and tell her he was fine and wasn't going home. He thought that once he figured out how to get around on the subway, he should have no problems at all. He had never been on a subway by himself, though he knew how to drive a car. He thought his pal Jack would certainly not mind taking him around the subways a few times, then he'd be all set for his new life. He wondered where Jack lived, thought maybe he could get a place near him. It certainly would help in the beginning to have a friend nearby.

The next morning when his friend returned home, they talked over coffee and donuts and looked through the classified ads in the *Village Voice* newspaper to see if there were any jobs he might be able to get. He made a few calls and got ready to set out for some interviews.

Then his host commented, "You really shouldn't go out on a job interview looking like that. Do you have any other clothes?"

Joe said he had another pair of slacks, but no jacket or shoes other than his sneakers.

"I'll tell you what. Before you go anywhere, I'll get you some clothes. When you get a job, you can pay me back," the other offered.

Joe agreed enthusiastically. He was so surprised and thrilled about his friend's generosity. Like a teenager going shopping with a loving father, Joe and the older man set out. Joe got himself a new jacket, a pair of stylish platform shoes, which added at least three inches to his height, a few fashionable shirts, and a Levi jacket. He looked like a different person. He had shed his out-of-town look and acquired a more mature and sophisticated appearance. He even got his hair cut, in a unisex style like Jack's. Joe and his "benefactor" had had a nice day. Of course, Joe didn't get to look for a job, but these were all preparations for getting a job. Joe had never before gotten so many clothes at one time. It was a day he would remember for a long time.

When they got back to the house, Jack called, inviting him over for dinner. Joe gladly accepted. While waiting for Jack to pick him up, he was told that some company was expected for the night and it would really be better if Joe stayed with Jack for the night. When Jack arrived, Joe asked him if he could stay for the night and Jack happily agreed. Joe packed some of his new clothes and left the apartment.

Jack lived in an attractive little studio apartment on the fashionable East Side. Joe was very impressed. For a 16½-year-old, Jack had done pretty well for himself. Jack's roommate was home. He was in his late twenties, a slim man with a beard and short cropped hair and was dressed only in his underwear. He looked a little like the friend who had bought Joe his new clothes. He greeted Joe warmly.

The apartment had only a few pieces of furniture—an immense couch, a few chairs and a table. Clothes were lying around all over. There was very little food in the refrigerator, so Jack's roommate suggested they check out the neighborhood bar, which also served hamburgers and sandwiches. With Joe's new wardrobe, he had no problem passing as eighteen, not that the place really cared about serving liquor to a minor. In the bar, they met someone Jack and his roommate knew, and all four returned to Jack's house for the night. Jack and his roommate pulled out a bed from the closet and Joe and the other man were given the large couch. Once they got into bed, Joe's bedmate made love to him. Joe had been too embarrassed and confused to say no. When Joe got up the next day, his bedmate had already left, leaving a twenty-dollar bill for Joe.

By now Joe was really puzzled about what was going on. In the first place, Jack was not "womanly" as Joe thought all homosexuals looked. In fact, he was thinking, that back home, the girls would love Jack. He dressed very well, in the latest style, and was very handsome. He liked Jack a lot and he didn't want to think anything bad about him. He could talk to Jack and Jack seemed to understand him. He wanted to stay friends. Jack noticed Joe's confusion. Jack decided to explain.

Jack began, "Man, let me tell you something, there ain't no jobs that you can get that will support you. The money that you could make wouldn't even pay for your rent. Do you like where I live? Well, that place would cost you about as much as you would make in a month."

"Well, I would like to try a few things anyway," Joe responded.

"Why don't you come with me to the place where I work," suggested Jack.

"What do you do?"

"I do lots of things. I'm a model and I act in some films. Maybe I can get you a job there, too."

Joe agreed. Jack was being a better friend to him than anyone had ever been. He really wanted to please Jack. He figured that maybe Jack had told the man that he needed money and that's why the man had left him the twenty dollars. He wanted to ask Jack, but didn't know how. Joe wanted to be like Jack. Jack had nice clothes and lots of friends, particularly adult friends, something that Joe found very impressive.

Joe had wondered what kind of clothes Jack was going to model but when they got to the place where Jack worked, Jack undressed. The photographer took pictures of him in various positions and gave him some money, and within an hour they were gone. Though surprised to learn what Jack had meant by "modeling," he tried to act as if he thought nothing of it. He didn't want Jack to think he was stupid. And Jack acted as if it were the most natural thing in the world. Joe wanted to know what the photographer was going to do with the pictures, but he decided not to ask.

"Joe, if you want, I'll introduce you to those guys. You can make as much money for an hour of that work, as working for days in a factory or a week at McDonald's. To-morrow I'll be making a film. If you like, I'll take you there with me too."

The next day they went to a dingy building on Ninth Avenue, in an area famous for prostitution and massage parlors. The building smelled of garbage and urine, and drunks were sitting or lying on the stoop, begging from people who walked by. Jack was the star of a thirty-five-minute pornographic film. Joe watched this, his best friend now, being made love to by a man he'd seen earlier dressed in leather from head to toe. He sensed there was something wrong with being in this place, watching a man make love to a boy to be filmed for Times Square consumption, but he didn't want to leave. He liked his friend, and he was afraid to leave. Jack received a hundred dollars for the day's work, a very impressive figure in Joe's estimation. He thought of his mother, who made about that much working as a waitress for a whole week. He wondered if he could do what his friend did. He didn't mind the nude photos, but making love in a film was very strange to him. He tried to rationalize it—maybe one can get used to it. He still wondered how Jack got into all this, but he didn't want to let on how weird this all was to him. He thought he should act "cool."

"I guess I'd do what you're doing, nude photos and stuff, but I'm not gay," explained Joe to his friend.

"I'm not gay either. I sleep with girls too. You know, the twenty dollars that man gave you that night? Well, you can make that much or more every night. That doesn't make you a faggot."

Hearing that certainly put Joe's mind at ease. He didn't like to think of himself as gay. If Jack wasn't gay and he still did this, then it couldn't be all that bad, he figured. He just didn't ever want to have to think of himself as anything but a man who sleeps with women.

"Well, how do you get into the movies?" he asked re-luctantly.

"My roommate will arrange all that when we get home. We'll talk to him. But you don't start with the movies. Plus you can't get a movie every day. My roommate finds guys for you, like the one who left you twenty dollars. He arranges all that. You don't have to worry about any of that. I'll teach you the rest of what you need to know," Jack assured him.

Just so Joe could see that Jack had girlfriends, they stopped by the house of a very attractive woman who was well into her twenties. Joe wondered what it would take for him to get a woman like that. He also wondered if she knew what Jack did for a living. If you could have a girlfriend like that, it would certainly be better if she didn't know you made love to men for money.

"We're all friends. I'll introduce you to some other of her friends. She does porn films too, and also works for my roommate. My roommate and the man who picked you up at Port Authority are partners. They are good friends. They get dates for a lot of guys. You'd be surprised how many guys are out there looking for dates. I'm sure that if you don't give them any trouble, they'll arrange for you as well."

Joe indicated that he would be no trouble. By now, this was becoming quite an adventure for Joe. Meeting people in bars, smoking pot, making lots of money—it was all so glamorous. They met with Jack's roommate who talked very fatherly to him.

"Listen, you have nothing to worry about. Jack will teach you a few things. I'll get the dates for you and make all the arrangements. I want to assure you that you needn't worry about a thing. Just do as you're told and you'll have no problems with us."

Joe started working for the two men. The nude photos and the films were to come after he was trained. He learned to pick up men in bars, in mens' rooms, and on street corners. He didn't make all the money Jack had promised though, because the men took their cut for making the arrangements.

Joe moved in with a young man who had the same occupation. Soon his friends, his whole world, revolved around his business. He got to know the gay bars, the hangouts, the porn stars, and the corner on Forty-second Street where boys are bought and sold like meat in the marketplace. For the most part, he had been treated well. Some guys were brutal—they liked to whip him—but most of them were middle-aged men looking for a companion for the night. According to Joe, many of the men were married. Some had children. Joe did what he was told. He was too scared not to follow orders. He had heard that Jack's roommate beat people up if they didn't follow orders, so he never tried to withhold money or not do what was expected of him.

By the time he was eighteen, he was thinking of really making a change in his life. But he didn't know what else he could do to make a living, and he was also afraid of trying to leave. He knew that some people had left without any trouble, but others the pimps had beaten up. But regardless of what they did to him, where would he turn for money, for friends? He had no trade, no profession, not even a high school diploma. At times, he was very depressed. He knew that he had to make money every night for his pimp, because if he didn't, he risked a beating or a whipping—or they could decide to do without him. It didn't seem anything like the kind of life that Jack had presented to him. He never got to do any movies, he only did a few photos, and most of the time he was out on the streets looking for men himself. He had already contracted VD a few times.

His friend Jack had left New York to live with an older man in Los Angeles. Jack knew the business well enough to realize that, as young as he was, he was old enough that his price would soon start going down. Joe wondered how he had found an older gentleman who would take care of him. That seemed to be the dream of many of the male prostitutes. He wondered what Jack had had to do to get that man. He knew

85

that he would never look as good as Jack; maybe it was out of the question for him. He also wondered about his family. Would they ever find out what he was doing to make a living?

Joe wrote his mother every six months or so just so she'd know he was alive. He never wrote his return address, only a post office box number. He was afraid that she would come to New York to look for him. He had always had nightmares from time to time, about his mother coming to New York and seeing him pick up a man on the street. He knew that she would die of shame.

He kind of felt sorry for his mother. She was all alone now. Joe's father was dead. Joe's mother had always worked as a waitress, six nights a week. Joe had worked at a gas station, and his sister, who was a year older, as a cashier in a store. Joe had run away one night while his mother was working and his sister was with her boyfriend. He had no clear idea of why he was running away. He liked his mother, though with her working at night, he hadn't really seen much of her, and though he fought with his sister a lot, he liked her too. But they had never gotten close either; she had always been out at night with some guy. He just had a feeling that "nothing was happening." He had no interest in school and got poor grades. He had had very few friends, and never fitted in too well at school. He hadn't been aggressive with the girls, so he had had no girlfriends. He had hated the fights that the guys got into. They called him a sissy, though he had never thought he was homosexual, and played jokes on him to embarrass him. He was just timid, and smaller than most of the other guys. He had a childish face, which got no attention from the girls. The guys used to beat him up a lot, and he hadn't fought back. He had learned to spend much of his time by himself, going to the movies, listening to records, or watching television. He loved to sit in front of the TV and daydream. He also liked to sleep a lot and get up late in the morning.

When he had left his hometown, he had had no idea of what

to expect. He had been in New York only a few times before, once with a group from school when they had spent their day around Times Square looking at peepshows. He just wanted to leave his town, find new friends, get a job, that's all. He had had no idea that the twelve dollars he took wasn't enough to get a hotel for a week. Actually, he hadn't thought it out at all. He just knew he wanted to leave and try his luck in a big city. If he could have quit school and gotten a good job he might not have left in the first place, but he had also wanted to meet some new people. Living in a small town became a bore. So he left.

He hadn't been home since then. He had always planned on going back, but was always afraid that his mother would somehow know that he was a male prostitute. Maybe his clothes were feminine and she'd be able to tell right away. He sent her birthday cards, sometimes a Christmas card. He had never really felt too close to anyone for any length of time, except Jack.

Joe loved to be with adults. It made him feel grown-up himself. Being with adults gave him a feeling of importance he had never known before. In the beginning, he had felt flattered that someone would want him enough to pay. That really surprised him. It was ironic to him that he could never get many girls even to go out with him, and now grown-up men payed to spend time with him. That gave him a bit of status.

Though nowhere nearly as frequently as girls, there are some male runaways who are forced to turn to prostitution for survival. Some of the males, like Joe, become male prostitutes out of ignorance and weren't homosexual, at least not to their knowledge, when they left home. Others, like Jack, ran away because they were already engaged in homosexual activities and were afraid their parents might find out. Jack knew that he enjoyed having sexual relations with his cousin, and because of his fine looks, he had already been approached

87

by several men by the time he was fifteen years old. He ran away because he had a sexual encounter with a teacher in school and was afraid that people would find out, particularly his parents. The teacher had given him some money to keep him quiet. He used the money to come to New York, where in no time at all he found men to support him. Within a week after he arrived in New York, he found his pimp in a mens' room in a Forty-second-Street movie house. The pimp introduced him to the porno film market. Jack turned tricks for a lot of money, and since he was such valuable property, his pimp wanted to watch him closely, so he moved him in with him. They got along well, and the pimps used Jack for many purposes. He recruited boys like Joe and many other lost teenagers who needed only a little push to enter the life of the homosexual prostitute. Jack was very good at convincing the young boys to join. Joe's feelings toward him were no different from those of many other kids. Jack was charming and a good listener, and always seemed to be a genuine friend. As it happened he liked Joe a lot, but many other kids thought he was their very best friend too, when with them he was just doing his job.

For many of the young men, this is merely a way to survive. They are not really homosexuals. They have girlfriends and the only time they engage in a homosexual act is for money, not for pleasure. Jack was bisexual. He slept with some men for pleasure, but he slept with women as well. He made money on both. He was not only good-looking but charming and lovable. He knew that sooner or later he would meet a wealthy older man who would support him.

There are pimps who live off their male prostitutes just as there are those who live off the females. However, most of the females are easier to control than the males. The boys like Joe are the ones they like to get a hold of. Joe was not nearly so sophisticated or charming as Jack. Joe was naive and ignorant of city life, so he was easy to manage. He would never cheat them of their share of the money and would be too scared ever to defy an order. Joe would be too scared to leave, because he would have no place to go. Joe was a good investment for them. He would work for them at least two or three years, then he would find something else to do in life. Bus terminals, train stations, public toilets are full of pimps. Some are looking to pick up females, while others are looking for young boys. Male prostitution is a very big business. While there are a lot more males prostituting themselves without a pimp than females, who seem to have a greater dependence on their pimp, a lot of the teenage boys work through pimps at least in the beginning. They often have someone like Jack who is close to their age, someone who will initiate them into the homosexual life if they are not already in it.

Because a runaway is often in a desperate emotional state, homosexual prostitution becomes not only a way to survive, but also a way to belong and be accepted by a group.

After two years of cruising and several cases of VD, Joe would have liked to get a regular job, but really didn't know how. He needed friends, and the only people he knew were those in the gay bars and movie houses. He had forgotten how to talk to "square" people, that is, people who have normal jobs, normal lives. Joe said he would be scared that a job interviewer might ask him what he had been doing for the past few years. What would he say? And how was he ever going to be able to start a relationship with a woman? He surely couldn't tell her what he did. He thought sometimes of leaving the city, giving up this life, but he wasn't ready for that yet.

There are many Joes and Jacks on the streets of big cities. In Houston not so many years ago, some thirty young boys were found murdered by a homosexual cultist group. Many of them were young runaways who had been picked up by a homosexual man who used them for sexual purposes and then killed them. Some of the same kind of kids are on the streets all over the United States. Some will be lucky enough to escape a tragic end, but others, like the boys in Houston, will meet a violent death when picked up by a man who wants more than sex.

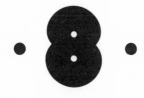

Returning Home

Before drawing a close to the research for the book, I decided to go out one more night with the runaway police unit to see if anything had changed. Were there fewer kids? Were they older or younger? Did they look any better? Well, things had changed very little. There is a new law in New York that makes it easier to arrest prostitutes, so there were fewer of them holding up the doorways, but otherwise, things remained the same as before. The male prostitutes were still on Fifty-third Street, the runaways were still out in Times Square and around Grand Central Station. The hotel where Karen Baxter was murdered seemed more desolate than ever, but that may have had to do with the fact that the city was trying to close down the hotel for fostering prostitution.

The evening was slow for the unit. Because of the large number of out-of-town tourists, it was hard to tell which ones were runaways and which were here with their parents. We moved along to all the familiar spots, looking harder than ever. Around 9:30 the officers called the bus terminal. With their newly received financial grant, the Port Authority police have been picking up kids at the speed of lightning. Sure enough, they had found somebody and needed the assistance of the city police.

Tonight, they had found Beth sitting in the waiting room frightened and lost. The officer had approached her just as a pimp sat down next to her. Beth had come all the way from her home in St. Louis with ten dollars. She had hitched rides to New Jersey and then taken a bus to New York. She was a pimp's dream. She was sixteen, but looked twelve or thirteen. She weighed less than a hundred pounds and was only four feet ten inches tall. She had long blond hair and blue eyes and wore no makeup. She looked as innocent as a baby.

This was not the first time she had run away. Just a month before, she had run to Kansas City, where her father and brother had gone to pick her up. Now, without a single piece of luggage, she had made it to New York. She wore a pair of jeans, a short-sleeved shirt, and a sweater. She didn't even have a change of clothes. She had a little purse filled with maps, cigarettes, a razor, and wads of Kleenex.

For the Port Authority police to have approached her when they did was to hit the jackpot. She had been in New York less than an hour, waiting for nobody, deciding what she should do next. The city police brought her into their office. She was stunned and bewildered. A social worker called her home. She had given her correct name, address, and telephone number. She was not yet slick enough to know that she could have lied. Her father, a stock broker, was at home. He immediately went to the airport to pay for her flight home. There were no more planes to St. Louis that night, so Beth was going to have to wait till the morning. All these transactions took place before she seemed to realize that her one-hour visit to New York was shortly coming to an end. Since neither the Port Authority police nor the runaway unit of the New York police wear uniforms, she apparently hadn't realized she was in the company of the police until they called her home and identified themselves as the police. She went with us without asking questions—just as she had gone with anyone else who came her way, the truck drivers, others who gave her rides, and just as she would have gone with a pimp. She was very lucky to be safe, but she didn't even know it.

The problem of where to place her for the night was serious. There is no place in New York where a runaway can go for just one night, so they are put in Spofford, noted for being a very rough institution meant to house children who are hardened, many of whom have committed serious crimes. This is where she was going to spend the night. No one wanted to put her there. Here was a tiny girl, who had never before spent a night in New York, who was about to stay with kids who have seen the very worst and have committed some of the worst crimes against themselves and society. We couldn't leave her at any of the runaway centers because they are not set up to handle people for one night. The centers feel that transients would destroy any type of structure. Moreover, the centers have no locked doors, and a kid can run away from them without any problem. Certainly, we couldn't risk letting her run away.

We all piled into the car and headed for the Bronx to take her to Spofford. She looked out the window asking what all the things were, wondering if we'd see the Empire State Building and were we going across a bridge. Going up the East Side, she wondered if it was the good part of New York. Her eyes were wide open; she didn't know which way to look first. We got up to Spofford and made all the arrangements. When we were ready to leave her, she looked as if she were going to say "How could you do this to me?" but all she said was "Good-bye." After we left, feeling a bit guilty for doing something to her that seemed so awful in our own minds, the officer who had treated her with such care and concern said, "I just hope everything will go all right tomorrow and she's taken to the airport without any trouble."

Driving back to Manhattan, around midnight, we all became silent. Then one of the officers said, "You know, I just hope that you put one thing in that book. I hope you say we shouldn't have had to put her in a place like that. She's not a criminal. She hadn't committed any crime. We need money to open up places where kids can be placed for the night that they can't run away from but where they won't be exposed to what they see at Spofford."

The night was over and she was scheduled to go home in the morning. It felt like true victory. The good guys had won. In a way it was funny—she didn't even know she had been saved. But we knew for sure that all anybody had to say to her was they'd give her a place to stay, and she would have been the new hooker on the block within the next two weeks.

After the officers talked to her mother and her social worker in St. Louis, it seemed that Beth and her mother were willing to work out their differences.

I asked GLIE for names of runaways who had returned home. I was delighted that the list was long. I chose Marie to call. She had returned to live with her mother after more than a year of absence.

"Well, I guess I came to my senses," Marie said. "I realized that there was nothing for me out there."

"Why did you leave in the first place?" I asked.

"Well, I used to have a lot of problems with my mother. She fought with me all the time and I got tired of it, so I left. Actually, what happened was that she worked a lot and wasn't home very much. I got into some things she didn't like, like my friends. We fought about a lot of little things like when I should be back from a party."

"When do you think that you should be home from a party?"

"I am fifteen years old and I feel that I should be able to make most of the decisions by myself. I guess about three in the morning is the right time to be in on the weekend. But my mother wanted me to be in by midnight. Most of the parties don't begin till ten o'clock. That really gives you no time at all. Then, she used to get mad because she would come home and I hadn't cooked the dinner or cleaned my room.

She'd forgotten that I had to go to school, I had a part-time job, and I wanted to spend some time with my friends."

As would be expected, Marie never mentioned that she had problems in school. She had failed a lot of subjects and was left back a year. Nor did she discuss how her mother must have felt about her daughter's hanging out with a bad group and coming home at three o'clock in the morning.

Of the year she was away, Marie spent over nine months in a runaway center. After she left the program they placed her into a foster home because she still didn't want to return home. After a few months with her foster parents, she decided to go home.

"What happened?" I asked.

"Well, I really didn't like it there. They didn't let me do anything. I figured that if someone was going to scream at me and tell me what to do, it might as well be my mother. So I came home."

"Do you get along with your mother now?"

"No, not really. We still fight a lot, but now I can take it a little better. She changed her ways a little and I changed mine. At least, I became more tolerant of her problems. She has a lot on her mind, trying to pay the bills and stuff. I understand that better now. I still don't agree that she should decide my friends for me or tell me what time I should be in the house. But I know that I can't support myself yet. I am saving my money, though."

"Do you think that you'll stay with your mother till you are eighteen?"

"No, I really doubt it. I am planning to work all winter and save my money so in a few years I can go and support myself."

Marie was typical of many of the teenagers I talked to. The way she saw the world was a mixture of reality and fantasy. While she was, in fact, working and saving a few dollars a week, she also had ideas of becoming a lawyer. When I pointed out to her that she'd better stay home for a while if she wanted to be a lawyer because that took many years of schooling and a lot of money, she regarded that fact very lightly. In fact, she had not thought about it at all. She seemed to think she was home for the time being only. It was possible she'd stay there, but she gave no indication that anything had really changed about her attitude toward home.

Many of the kids who returned home voiced similar feelings. Home still had a lot of problems, but they were going to stay there for a while because they had come to realize that the life of a runaway can be awfully cold and lonely. Many of the runaways who went home did so with a great deal of help from programs that counseled both them and their parents. But they returned without illusions. Some of the arguments remained, but both the parents and the kids had learned to handle them a little better. Almost all the teenagers I talked to were certain that by the time they are fifteen, they could handle all the problems that could be sent their way. They all thought that they should be able to stay out past midnight. Most of them viewed their parents as old-fashioned and strict. While they were all ready to take on the world, most of them had no idea how much rent their parents paid or how much food costs. They all told me they could live on hamburgers from McDonald's very easily, and they cost less than fifty cents. The kids who worked spent most of their money on clothes, records, and entertainment. Some of them saved a little money, but none had more than would be used up in a few days if they were trying to survive by themselves.

For some of the kids, the streets had taught them a lesson and they went home.

"I know one thing. I'm not going to run away again," said Frank, a fourteen-year-old from Boston.

"It's not that everything is OK at home, it's just that I realized that I am going to have to wait a little longer before I can make it on my own. At first I really liked it. I stayed out about three weeks before they caught me. After the second or third week, I began to get scared. I missed my friends

96

but I couldn't call them because I was afraid they would tell my mother. I felt like a fugitive. So when the street worker from a program found me in a park, I was very ready to come home. I just hadn't known how. I was really scared to come back to my parents' house. I knew they would beat me up and scream at me. But this counselor from a center had called, and I was glad, because he must have said some things to my folks, because they didn't beat me up. They just yelled a lot. Anyhow, I've been back for a while and now I can stand them better. There are still a lot of the same things that I don't like but I'd rather be here and listen to some of the things they say than be out there by myself. As they say, I learned my lesson and now I'm trying to get along with them until I can go to work and make it on my own."

While the runaway problem is still serious and a lot of kids are still running away, a lot of them are also going back home, often with the help of programs designed to service youth in need of help. Every day more and more people are becoming aware that spending a billion dollars a year on the juvenile justice system is not the answer. We need a lot more legislation like the Runaway Youth Act.

The Tom Sawyer and Huck Finn runaway stories are in the past. Kids will no longer run away to rivers that are within a half mile of their homes. Stories of runaways will no longer generate the excitement of the hippie movement of the sixties, representing a mass denial of a way of life. The runaway stories that we will be left with will be like the ones presented in this book. This book is dedicated to the idea that with more information gathered, more money allocated, and more action taken, many of the problems presented here will become like the dinosaurs—extinct. It is written with the hope that from here on, we can write about youth who are productive and who are working toward a better society and a better way of life for all of us. Let us invest not only in stocks of oil and steel, but also in the most valuable stock of all, our children.

A Time to Make Changes

It is no longer possible to run away and not fear the dangers of the city. Running to the big city was probably always fraught with the hardships of finding a way to live, loneliness, and desolation. Today we have to add the risks—which always existed but are greater today—of both becoming a victim of crime and of being sucked in to a life of crime. The friendly guy who offers a child a place to stay turns out to be a pimp. The pregnant woman who buys you a cup of coffee is not pregnant at all and works for the same pimp that you will. The cheap hotel where you can afford a night's rest is a center for drug traffic, a place for the prostitutes to take their clients. That out-of-town look attracts bad people like flies—people who want to make as much money on you as they possibly can.

Not only have the conditions of society changed, but the teenagers have changed as well. Not long ago, a child was seen but not heard. Kids clearly understood their place in the home and in society. They obeyed their parents and there was no such thing as children's rights. Children were often isolated from adult problems and discussions and free to concern themselves with only their teenage problems. Also, with less moving around, the kids knew each other better. They knew whom they could trust and who would squeal on them.

Now most of those ways are no more than a memory of the past—if not a very distinct past, an irretrievable one. Now, teenage girls worry about not forgetting to take their birth control pills, not getting VD, and having enough money to buy the latest fashions. They are aware of the confused state of the society, the contradictions and confusions that adult life offers. They are no longer treated as children, their opinions about the family's most important decisions are heard. They have seen their parents split up, their fathers or mothers replaced by new men or women. Being a teenager today is not what it used to be. It's more like being an adult of the twentieth century. The young are involved in the adult world, and they are asked to make adult decisions. Therefore, it should be no surprise that they feel they can govern their lives without their parents' supervision. They can live alone, they think.

The roles of either the parent or the adolescent are no longer very clear. A parent is no more than a financial provider for most children past the age of twelve or thirteen. Often they no longer give very much advice to their children or know very much about their children's lives. Both spend a minimum amount of time at home and of the little time spent together, it is seldom spent talking. Watching television has become the perfect excuse for being in the same room with someone, but not having to say a word to him or her. Most adolescents receive their advice from their peers, and it's with them that they share their secrets. However, that usually means being a part of a gang or a group, which may in turn mean drinking with the group or smoking a joint of marijuana to be accepted. The group may even be involved in vandalism, car theft, or breaking windows and stealing.

Within the last twenty-five years we have seen the age-old custom of the extended family dissolve into the nuclear family, and from that into the divorced woman with far too many children to handle alone. All over the world, the family had always consisted of a mother, a father, cousins, aunts, uncles, grandparents, nephews, and nieces, and they all lived close and saw one another often. They were supportive of each other both emotionally and financially. Very often, an adolescent turned to a grandparent for help and advice. The role of the grandparent had been a very important function. Many of the things you couldn't tell your parents, you could tell your grandma or grandpa. Now families are scattered, and the traditional extended family is all but absent from society.

Although we have no absolute or all-encompassing answers to the question of why children and young people run away, there are certain trends that we can observe. There is no doubt that the breakdown of the family, divorce and separation, and the problems of the alcoholic or abusive parent have a lot to do with it. For many of the female runaways with whom I spoke, working mothers are also a factor. They have had to take on the burdens of their overworked mothers—numerous children, bills, and chores. Clearly, most of the runaways come from homes that are filled with unhappiness and hopelessness. Some of the kids feel that they are a burden, that it's too hard for the parents to feed them, clothe them. They feel that their family would be better off without them. Frequently such kids are also those who are in some degree of trouble at school or with the law. There seems to be a direct relationship between a kid not doing well in school or playing hookey and his or her getting in trouble. It seems that if a kid does not have a firm base in school, they have very few places to turn to but to the other kids who are also doing poorly in school. Then together they start getting into mischief—or real crime.

Then there are the kids whose running away is a cry for help. In these situations there are usually a lot of problems that have been avoided and remained unresolved. When a child leaves, it is often to bring the attention of the parents to the fact that they must address the problem directly and stop sweeping it under the rug. Often, those families are economically better off. The father may be immersed in his work and the mother occupied with numerous social events. A lot of these kids go to sleepaway camps in the summer and spend the rest of the year keeping company with the maid or housekeeper. Perhaps they want to say they feel ignored and unloved. Sometimes the kids get into all kinds of bizarre activities just to get their parents' attention.

There is a lot of pressure on an adolescent. Pressure to please the parents and pressure to belong to a group and take part in activities—even ones you might not want to have anything to do with. The conflict between peer pressures and parental guidance also contributes to some young people's decision to leave.

Often the values that are promoted at home and the values that exist among the group are in conflict; the confusion can have a very serious effect on an adolescent. Some young people have a deep-seated need to be accepted by a group, yet they would also like to please their parents. When they can't find a happy medium they either defy their parents and do things that they are not permitted to do, getting in trouble at home, or they have few friends and spend much of their time at home alone. They don't get invited to the Saturday night events, they get teased at school, and soon they feel resentful.

Some of these kids come from very strict homes with domineering fathers. These families tend to be very old-fashioned in their outlook toward their female children especially, imposing the type of discipline that makes it hard for the girls to participate in a peer group. Many of the runaways made the decision to leave home after relatively minor events, such as getting a severe punishment after coming home late. Clearly they had been unable to resolve the conflict. Of course, a strong-minded child can handle these problems a lot better.

101

They are not as anxious to please either their parents or a peer group. They have a sense of direction of their own and find refuge in their own activities.

Some kids are always going to run away. The problem has been on the rise and will most probably increase for some time. More and more, American families are faced with critical problems at home, as well as ones in the economic, social, and psychological sphere. Hardship is transferred to the kids and many of them decide to leave rather than stay home and watch what might be a destructive situation. The problem of the teenage runaway is part of the same problem that causes families to break apart. As divorce and poverty and the need for welfare recede—if ever they do—so will the problem of the teenage runaway.

It is not easy to improve living conditions or increase a society's sanity, and that's perhaps what it would take to make our homes happier. But even before that is achieved the teenager's identity problems, hopelessness, and excess energy could be better dealt with.

Psychologists, anthropologists, and sociologists have recognized for a long time that adolescence presents certain difficulties. It is a time when a person is no longer a child, but has not yet fully matured into adulthood. In many societies it is treated as a time of special preparation for adulthood—a time to learn to hunt or herd cattle, to gather roots or work the field. Many cultures celebrate this age with rites of passage, special ceremonies, or initiation practices, marking the transition from one stage in life to the next. It is during this time that the children take on the values of that society and learn to carry on tradition. They are taught and watched, carefully guided into adulthood. They are offered the philosophy of the culture, spending much of their time with their peers but given complete guidance from the elders. It is important to the culture that they become respectable citizens because they are considered the product of that society. They are the next generation.

102

If we no longer have the close-knit extended family, or even the mother, father, and children together, we have to find new institutions. Just as children need to go to school to learn math and science, they also need a place to go to learn values and the more abstract skills of getting along in this world. And if their homes are inadequate for the purpose or down-right harmful, they need somewhere else to turn for that knowledge—somewhere other than the street gangs and groups which so often today are serving the purpose. We need some place like GLIE, Group Live In Experience, the community service program in the Bronx we discussed earlier. GLIE not only deals with the kid who ran away, but it also helps the entire family with other problems, ranging from alcoholism to housing.

When I went to see the former home of Karen Baxter, the fifteen-year-old runaway who was murdered in a sleazy hotel in New York, I could see why she wanted to run away. She had lived in a tenement where most of the windows were broken, where it was dark and frightening even to go in, where the hallways were dirty and uninviting. Her mother still lived there with the other children and a granddaughter, the baby of her other teenage daughter. I talked to Karen's eleven-year-old brother. A very sweet-looking kid, he said his mother still cried when people brought up Karen's name. He said she was always exhausted from working so late at night. Karen's brother was going to be placed in a foster home, because he's what is called "getting into trouble," and his mother's nerves were so bad she couldn't deal with him anymore. Karen's running away was obviously an escape from such conditions. After that, who knows what her motives were.

There have to be places where the Karens can go—youth hostels, residences, homes, where a teenager can move in and receive guidance and assistance from adults at least until they turn eighteen. They shouldn't have to turn to the streets for survival, and at fifteen, they shouldn't be forced to give up hope on the legitimate way of life, leaving them no place to turn to but crime.

We spend a fortune on "juvenile jails" or reform schools. It would seem far more useful to make available the help needed to shape our young into healthy adults while they are still undestroyed by the street life.

We are fortunate that today's youth are for the most part healthy and well developed. But that health generates a fantastic amount of energy, which is often misplaced, which needs to be channeled properly. Why couldn't we let the kids rebuild our tenements? Reconstruct the decaying houses? Let us develop youth organizations through which they can help the elderly, run errands for them, go for walks with them and gain their wisdom and knowledge. Let them help make our parks and zoos beautiful and teach them about ecology, our relationship with nature. We could send them out west to help the farmers. They would love it. We need to help them turn their immense energies into constructive, valuable things in life, making them feel useful at the same time. We must redefine their role and remind ourselves of their usefulness in our society. They can't just be parasites, particularly at a time when economic conditions are bad. It is insane that the young people can't find jobs when they want to work, they want to learn, and they hate having to resort to crime for survival. It is clearly in the best interest of the government to keep these kids busy and working, rather than have to spend a fortune on locking them up in jails.

The changes would have to be major ones—we cannot expect miraculous results from a few minor changes. But it seems to me our young people are worth it, unless we are willing for large numbers of our teenagers to be angry and violent, spending much of their time in court or in reformatories, both of which cost the taxpayers tremendous sums. More significantly, it also costs our youth, because the government doesn't have money left for youth centers, recreation areas, and ball parks. To permit the high-crime situation to go on is the most expensive of all alternatives available to us. It would cost far less to open up a community center every mile or so in urban areas, where teenagers can meet, play ball, organize teams, run track, and swim, working off their energy, and having a meeting place with adult supervision. This seems more logical than spending our money on the courts and reform schools, or leaving the kids on the streets to terrorize the old folks and destroy their own future.

But no matter how many preventive measures are taken, some kids will always run away—some may be better off leaving. And these kids need a place to stay—properly supervised homes, not institutions—where they can finish their adolescence without fear and violence. Perhaps we need to get away from having our biological parents as the only source of support and guidance. Perhaps we need to spread out the responsibility for child care among a larger group of adults, as in the old days when the extended family was responsible for child rearing. Maybe we need to help some of the parents, relieve them of some of the responsibility, as is done in the Israeli kibbutzim where the children are separated from their parents and live communally, receiving guidance and direction from professional child care specialists.

Unfortunately, most of our children's shelters have been large institutions marked by a multitude of problems, and where proper supervision and care have been absent. Those are not the kind of institutions we need for our youth. Those places only destroy their spirit and teach them how to be "bad." Rather, there is a need for small units, in small houses, with an atmosphere of home, a place where the young people can feel loved and wanted, where adult guidance is available. The runaways who have unsuitable homes, or the urban nomads who are unwanted at home, should have alternatives. Their lives should not be doomed to misery, hardship, and crime even before they reach adulthood.

It is up to us to change our priorities and place our efforts on our future stock so that they can learn to lead this country and go in the direction of progress, not destruction. We must take responsibility for our youth collectively, rather than leave the responsibility to individual parents. And we must do it before thousands of young lives are damaged beyond repair.

Fortunately, some programs do exist, which are serving our youth with dedication and care. And fortunately the Runaway Youth Act, or as some call it, "the Birch Bayh Bill," was passed in 1974, providing aid to agencies to operate temporary-shelter programs in areas where runaways tend to gather and to provide counseling and medical services where needed.

According to Senator Bayh, the bill was based on the realization that "these shelters can divert young people from our failing juvenile system and prevent them from resorting to criminal acts which can easily lead to a life of crime." In response to the astonishing statistics that the juvenile justice system costs over $1 billion a year, a sum that is increasing at the unbelievable rate of $50 million a year, the act authorized spending $10 million per year for three years to run the centers. Of the $10 million, Congress appropriated $6 million, $7 million, and $9 million to be spent in 1974, 1975, and 1976, respectively. At the time this book is being published, January 1977, the bill will be up for extension, which, the senator's office says, the coming administration is very much in favor of.

It makes sense to implement these programs even for the cost factor alone. By far the most expensive institutions are those in which juveniles are incarcerated for long periods. In those, the average annual cost per youth is $7,500; far higher than the average per-person cost of a halfway house or group home—only $2,500 per year. But beyond the cost factor, the rate of recidivism, the tendency to relapse into the criminal behavior, among juveniles has been estimated at 74 to 85 percent. On any given day, there are 8000 juveniles held in jails in the United States and it is estimated that more than

100,000 youths spend one or more days each year in adult jails. And many of those are runaways.

As Bayh put it, "The problem of the youthful criminal offender is often related to the runaway problem. Many youngsters, soon after leaving their homes, find themselves in circumstances where they resort to illegal activities, including prostitution and drug pushing, in order to support themselves or are similarly victimized by criminals young and old. The Runaway Youth Act can with continued adequate funding stop this vicious cycle before it can begin."

Well over three hundred applications for funding are pending. Clearly, there is great demand for the money. There is hope that now, finally, a movement for putting our youth back on the right track is under way. The Bayh committee has done its share in the effort. Nine million dollars isn't much compared with the billions spent on the juvenile justice system annually. Let's hope the investment of the much smaller amount will effect a rapid reduction of the need for the larger.

Index

About the Author

Anna Kosof, an anthropologist, has long been interested in the impact of the stress of modern society on the individual—especially it's effect on women. In the course of researching a manuscript on female drug addicts, Ms. Kosof met many female runaways. And so her interest in the plight of runaways, of both sexes, was sparked.

Presently, Ms. Kosof is general manager of radio station WBAI in New York City.